A selection from

Human Action
a Treatise on Economics

by Ludwig von Mises

selected and assembled by Gérard Dréan

About this book

The body of this book is a selection of paragraphs from Ludwig von Mises' "Human Action, a treatise on economics", arguably one of the most important books ever written in the area of economics.

Rather than attempting to summarize Mises' thought in different words, it uses Mises' own words and sentences, selected and reassembled in such a way that it can hopefully serve as a summary of the fundamentals and as an introduction to Mises' work.

The source for this selection is the fourth edition of Human Action (1996), available in electronic format from the Internet site of the Ludwig von Mises Institute (www.mises.org). Every paragraph in the selection comes unchanged from the original text. A few long paragraphs have been shortened or broken down to facilitate reading. Redundant paragraphs in different chapters of the original work have been eliminated. The resulting selection has been reorganized for logical flow and readability of the resulting text.

The chapter and section number of the paragraph in the original book are indicated between square brackets at the end of each paragraph. Modern typographic conventions are used where they differ from the original.

Contents

Preface

Human Action, a treatise on economics is the magnum opus of Ludwig von Mises, the central author of the so-called "Austrian" tradition of economics. The present book is a selection from *Human Action*, prepared in the hope of spreading the knowledge of that monumental and at the same time unrecognized work.

The Austrian school of economics

The phrase "Austrian school" usually stands for an economic tradition starting with Carl Menger (1840-18211921), one of the three founding fathers of marginalism with Léon Walras and William Stanley Jevons. Its main authors are Eugen von Böhm-Bawerk (1851-1914), Friedrich von Wieser (1851-1926), Ludwig von Mises (1881-1973), Friedrich von Hayek (1899-1992) and Ludwig Lachmann (1906-1990), all of Austrian nationality and directly or indirectly students of Menger. Joseph Schumpeter (1883-1950) may to a certain extent be considered as a fellow traveler of that school, which also includes American economists such as Murray Rothbard (1926-1995) and Israel Kirzner (born 1930).

The Austrian school is generally considered as a mere variety of marginalism, or as that wing of neoclassical economic theory which is most opposed to state intervention. Actually, the Austrian school differs fundamentally from neoclassical "mainstream" economics by its very conception of the discipline and of the methods appropriate to its substance. For instance, it rejects the model of the rational and omniscient

homo economicus, it studies the processes of change and not equilibrium, rejects the separation between macroeconomics and
microeconomics, and considers the use of mathematical reasoning as not only inappropriate but harmful. Because of those
positions, the Austrian school is very much a minority
nowadays. Hayek's name is known but disparaged for his "ultra
liberalism", but Mises is hardly ever quoted or mentioned by
professional economists; academic manuals seldom mention
his name, and many histories of economic thought dismiss him
in a couple of paragraphs at best, or simply ignore the man and
his work. When he is mentioned, his work is most of the time
grossly misrepresented. At the same time, many of his earnest
readers regard him as one of the greatest economists of the
twentieth century, if not the greatest.

Now the epistemological and methodological positions
that characterize the Austrian school, which are thoroughly ex-
pounded in *Human Action*, are identical with those that have
prevailed from the origins of economic thought until the end
of the nineteenth century. In a wider historical perspective,
freed from the optical illusion that makes us mistake the tree of
contemporary mainstream economics for the forest of economic thought of all times, one can on the contrary view "neoclassical" economics (a misnomer) as a disproportionate but
pathological excrescence of a truly "main" stream running
from Democritus and Aristotle to the Austrians through the
Spanish scholastics of the sixteenth century, the French classical school of Cantillon, Turgot, Condillac, Say and Bastiat,
with *Human Action* as one of its culminating points.

Except for believing blindly that the so-called "mainstream" has completely and definitely made obsolete all earlier
economic thought, the study of economics must make room
for the authors of the Austrian tradition. Moreover, the insights of Austrian economists on topics such as market processes, money or economic cycles deserve at any rate serious
consideration, at a time when the attending policy recommend-
ations find a renewed interest after the blatant failure of real
socialism and the challenging of the conventional Keynesian
ideas. Finally, the Austrian tradition provides a far more solid
methodological foundation for the study of the enterprise and

industrial structures than does the neoclassical paradigm, as exemplified by the "evolutionary" school.

The Austrian economic tradition, started by Carl Menger in 1871, enjoyed a remarkable development in the first three decades of the twentieth century, then split into various sub currents, one of which merged into the dominant neoclassical mainstream while the other fell into marginality, until Mises attempted to bring it back to the forefront.

Menger, generally associated with Léon Walras and William Stanley Jevons in the invention of marginalism, was actually proposing a basically different idea of economics as a discipline. Both Walras and Jevons wanted to create a new science: Walras by imitating the science of mechanics in order to propose a theory of general equilibrium; Jevons, followed by Marshall, by proposing a theory of partial equilibriums. In both cases, the subject of the study was situations where economic actions have produced all their effects and where time is suspended, using an *ad hoc* model of human beings, the famous rational and omniscient *homo œconomicus*.

Menger, like his classical predecessors, teaches that economics is the study of cause-effect relationships between phenomena that unfold in time and stand little chance of ever reaching equilibrium situations. The study of economic equilibriums, the very definition of economics for Walras, is for Menger a very ancillary issue.

Menger also opposes the German Historical School, that maintains that there are no general laws of economic phenomena. Menger draws a distinction between history, the study of particular events, and economics, the study of general laws that govern the particular events. Both are legitimate: the division of tasks between scientific disciplines is a form of division of labour for understanding the world, the explanation of every event requiring the totality of human knowledge. He develops those epistemological and methodological conceptions in "*Untersuchungen über die Methode der Sozialwissenschaften, und der politischen Ökonomie insbesondere*" (*Investigations into the method of the social sciences*, 1882).

Of the first two disciples of Menger's, Böhm-Bawerk and Wieser, the latter leans rapidly towards a reconciliation with the general equilibrium theory, a path where such authors as Schumpeter and Hayek will follow him to different degrees. Wieser's position becomes dominant after he succeeds Menger at the Vienna University in 1902, then after Böhm-Bawerk's death in 1914 and Menger's in 1921. Soon, trying to escape the rise of Nazism in the thirties, Austrian economists take refuge in the Anglo-Saxon world, dominated by marshallian ideas, and many set about to merge their own insights with the equilibrium theories. That part of Menger's thought which opposes Walras and Jevons falls into oblivion.

Ludwig von Mises has remained a faithful disciple of Menger and Böhm-Bawerk. His first significant work addresses precisely a topic that does not find a place in the different theories of equilibrium: money and credit[1]. After serving as an artillery officer in World War I, he resumes his position as first secretary of the Vienna Chamber of Commerce, where he first opposes successfully the inflationist tendencies of the government, but can only postpone until 1931 the complete collapse of the currency and of the economy which had hit Germany as soon as 1923.

At the same time, being both Jewish and a vocal opponent to any form of totalitarianism, he views with extreme concern the rise of communism in Russia and of National Socialism in Germany. He then intensifies the fierce intellectual fight that he has engaged against statism in all its forms, from communism to Nazism, with *Die Wirtschaftsrechnung im sozialistischen Gemeinwesen* (Economic Calculation in the Socialist Commonwealth) in 1920, *Die Gemeinwirtschaft* (Socialism) en 1922 and *Liberalismus* (Liberalism) in 1927. In 1934, he accepts a teaching assignment in Geneva, and has to emigrate to the US in 1940 because of the Nazi threat.

Mises is then convinced that ignorance and wrong theories are the source of many troubles that humanity inflicts upon itself: the inflationary monetary practices of the states, and the

1 *Theorie des Geldes und der Umlaufsmittel* (1912)

theories that pretend to justify them, are leading to disaster; socialism, and even all forms of economic interventionism, however attenuated, are leading to the ruin of civilization. He sets for himself the task of eradicating all those errors by exposing the economic phenomena in their totality.

In Geneva, relieved from his official responsibilities, he spends the better part of five years consolidating, extending and structuring his views into a complete integrated theory of economic phenomena: *Nationalökonomie,* a one thousand page book published in 1940 and in German, which was not the best combination of date and language for its recognition; the war actually prevented its distribution, and his Swiss publisher went bankrupt. During his exile in the USA, Mises prepared an English-language version, which was published in 1949 as *Human Action, A Treatise on Economics.*

Human Action

Human Action is very different from other economic treatises, by its tone as well as by its construction. It is at the same time a militant book by its passionate defence of a realist conception of economic science and of individual freedom, a didactic book which addresses everybody and not only professional economists, and nevertheless a scholarly book demanding a lot from the reader and following the reasoning up its remote consequences. In this book, Mises synthesises and extends his prior works, making it "the precipitate of half a century of experience", in other words a genuine sum of economic knowledge.

Convinced that many errors that he wants to expose originate in an erroneous conception of economic science, he goes through the task of placing economics in the context of the other sciences, as Menger did and as he himself had already done in 1933 in *Grundprobleme der Nationalökonomie* (Epistemological Problems of Economics).

He also remains true to the classics, who had already remarked that economics as a discipline is radically different from the physical sciences: experimentation is impossible, but the basic phenomena are directly accessible to us. John Elliott

Cairnes summarized it in 1857: *"If the economist was at a disadvant-age as compared with the physical investigator in being excluded from ex-periment, he had also some compensating circumstances on his side... The economist starts with a knowledge of ultimate causes. He is already, at the outset of his enterprise, in the position which the physicist only attains after ages of laborious research."*[2]

Jean-Baptiste Say prophesized already in 1803 that when the economic science would be perfected and disseminated, « *A treatise on political economy will then be reduced to a small number of principles, that will not even need, to be supported by proof, because they will be nothing else but the statement of what everybody knows, arranged in a suitable order to grasp their totality and their relations*[3]. »

The economist's task consists therefore first of establish-ing a certain number of undeniable facts, then drawing the consequences by mere logical deduction. If those starting ax-ioms are well chosen and if they are undeniably true, and if the logical reasoning is correct, the consequences drawn from them will also be undeniably true.

Mises starts from the established fact that the ultimate cause of economic phenomena is the action of human beings. It is therefore in the study of human action that economics must find its founding principles: laws of action that must be truly general, that apply to all actions irrespective of the cir-cumstances and content of each particular action.

That conception of economic science is that of Menger. It is at the same time abstract and realist: abstract because it does not take into account all the characteristics of real human be-ings and of their actions, but only those that are common to certain classes of situations. It is realist because the character-istics taken into account are effectively present in real human beings. They are even what distinguishes the human species

2 The Character and Logical Method of Political Economy

3 *Un traité d'économie politique se réduira alors à un petit nombre de principes, qu'on n'aura pas même besoin d'appuyer de preuves, parce qu'ils ne seront que l'énoncé de ce que tout le monde saura, arrangé dans un ordre convenable pour en saisir l'ensemble et les rapports (*Traité d'économie politique, Discours préliminaire)

from all others, conscience and intentional action, contrary to the assumptions constituting *homo œconomicus*, that have absolutely nothing human.

But human action occurs in areas that extend largely beyond economy. Mises is thus led to consider economics as a branch of « praxeology », the science of human action as such, independently of the motives and forms of action, that belong to the area of psychology. Here again, as in Menger, the distinctions that he draws between sciences define a division of work, but in no way implies a hierarchy or exclusion.

For Mises, the entire economic science rests upon a small number of axioms, which derive their truth from our knowledge of ourselves as human beings, and are therefore *a priori* truths. The first of those truths is "men act", an undeniable fact since negating it would already be an action. In *Human Action*, Mises shows that the "action axiom" implies in a necessary way the categories of ends, means, causality, uncertainty, time preference, and, step by step, those of value, cost, interest, etc., eventually generating the whole economic theory. One cannot help thinking of Descartes, who constructed his entire philosophy from his *cogito, ergo sum*.

In the twentieth century, that view of economics as a purely deductive science based on *a priori* axioms, on the same ground as logic and mathematics, has become sufficiently original and misunderstood to lead Mises to devote essentially the first ten chapters (over 200 pages) to justifying and explaining it, before moving to the area that is generally considered as that of economics.

That conception of the economic discipline, at the opposite of neoclassical epistemology, which takes the physical sciences as a model, would suffice to discredit Mises in the eyes of mainstream economists. But its logical consequences, that Mises develops over more than five hundred pages in the fourteen chapters that follow, are no less opposed to the dominant ideas. In contrast with the fictitious world of static equilibrium and perfect information of neoclassical theory, Mises maintains that economics is meaningless if it does not account for the passage of time and for the radical uncertainty resulting from the limited knowledge of acting man. He teaches that there are no constant relations in economic phenomena, and therefore that no measurements are possible. His economics is a qualitative discipline where mathematics have no useful place, while mainstream economics see the use of mathematics as the very prerequisite for its scientific status.

Having thus analyzed the principles and the operation of economic phenomena, Mises then tackles the interventionist doctrines, before concluding on the place of economics in knowledge and its relationship with the essential problems of human existence in the last three chapters.

In total, that monumental work presents an original conception of the discipline, together with developments on most of its fundamental problems. It covers a wide range of topics, from the epistemological foundations to the ethical, political and social issues, including a theory of indirect exchange, a theory of money and capital, a theory of the market, a theory of economic cycles, and much more.

Human Action is one of the highest points of economic thought of all times. In scope and depth, it can only be compared to Say's *Traité d'Economie politique*, with which it has a lot in common, to John Stuart Mill's *Principles*, or to Marx' *Das Kapital*, of which it is the antithesis. It is more complete than *The Wealth of Nations*, where Smith takes epistemology for granted, or than Marshall's *Principles of Economics*, which remains close to the principles level and does not go as far into such topics as capital theory or political considerations.

This selection: why and how

One problem remains: *Human Action* contradicts many of the dogmas of "standard economics". In order to follow Mises, one has to accept that a good share of what is presented as economic science in the twentieth century is only a meaningless intellectual amusement.

Overcoming the economists' prejudice against Mises is therefore a formidable endeavor. Even when I occasionally manage to persuade one that *Human Action* is worth his reading, one obstacle still remains: the sheer size of the book, which is a formidable deterrent for reluctant would-be readers. I therefore imagined that an effective way to contribute to the dissemination of Mises' thought would be to present its fundamentals in a more concentrated way.

Rather than writing a summary, I believed that it would be better to use Mises' own words and sentences. So I set out to select and assemble pieces of *Human Action* in such a way that it could serve as a summary of the fundamentals and as an introduction to Mises' work. I decided to choose as a unit the paragraph rather than the sentence, because one paragraph generally corresponds to a natural level of elaboration of one idea. Also, full paragraphs convey a better image of Mises' style than individual sentences.

The selection aims to remain by and large at the level of definitions and clarification of concepts, leaving out further elaboration and detailed discussion of specific issues. For instance, significant space is devoted to the definition of economics as a discipline, but most of the discussion of the socialist economy and of the mixed economy (chapters XXV to XXXVI) is left out, as well as personal criticism of other economists.

The selection has been reorganized regardless of the original sequence, the sole criteria being consistency, logical flow and readability of the resulting text. That led to eliminate more redundancies, since the same idea is often repeated in a different form in different places of the full text, as a reminder of earlier discussions.The final text is structured into short subsections, each dealing with a limited topic and carrying a self-explanatory title, most of the time a title or subtitle of the original work to facilitate reference. The chapter and section number of the paragraph in the original book are indicated between square brackets at the end of each paragraph.

Very few personal comments have been added as footnotes, for example the definition of difficult terms when they have not yet been defined in the text, which only happens in a couple of places. All the footnotes in the original text have been eliminated; in the few cases where text from an original footnote by Mises had to be retained, it has been included in the main text of this selection.

The structure of this selection

The final result is structured in eight chapters. The order of exposition follows roughly that of the original work: first, an analysis of human action in general and of the nature of the economic discipline in relation with the other sciences, then the study of human actions in the particular area of economics, and finally the political implications.

The first two chapters gather developments about the economic science per se. Chapter 1 covers the place of economics in the sciences, and the differences and relations between the physical sciences and the human sciences. It matches roughly chapters I (Acting man), II (The Epistemological Problems of the Sciences of Human Action) and III (Economics and the Revolt Against Reason) of the original book. It includes excerpts from chapters XIV (The Scope and Method of Catallactics) and XXXIX (Economics and the Essential Problems of Human Existence).

Chapter 2 covers the characteristics of economics as a discipline, and the specific methods appropriate to that field of study. It matches primarily chapters XIV (The Scope and Method of Catallactics), XVI (Prices) and XXXVIII (The Place of Economics in Learning) of the original book.

Chapter 3 addresses the study of human action in general. It defines methodological individualism as the thought discipline which enables to account for all forms of social constructs and processes. It reviews the goals and conditions of human action, which always aims at exchanging the present situation for a future situation considered as more satisfactory. Value and profit are thus defined in a general and strictly subjectivist way, as well as man's attitude towards time, uncertainty, rationality and freedom. The division of labor is presented as an essential feature of human society. This chapter 3 of the selection corresponds roughly to chapters IV (A First Analysis of the Category of Action), V (Time), VI (Uncertainty), VII (Action Within the World) and VIII (Human Society) of the original work, with passages from chapters XV (The market) and XVIII (Action in the Passing of Time).

Chapters 4 to 7 cover economics proper. Money is introduced in chapter 4, first as a means of indirect exchange, then as a means of economic calculation. The value of money is discussed based on the demand for money on one hand, the supply of money and money substitutes on the other hand. Economic calculation is introduced as the tool used by entrepreneurs to adjust their actions to the desires of their fellow men. This chapter 4 of the selection corresponds to chapters XI to XIII of the original book, which form Part Three (Economic Calculation), and chapter XVII (Indirect Exchange).

Chapter 5 is about the importance of time in economics. It presents time preference and originary interest as essential praxeological facts. It shows the difference between capital goods, which are products set aside for future production, and their valuation in monetary terms, which is the base for capital accounting. It corresponds to chapters XVIII (Action in the Passing of Time), XIX (Interest) and XX (Interest, Credit Expansion, and the Trade Cycle) of the original book.

Chapter 6 expands the theory of money and capital into a theory of economic cycles. This chapter is entirely taken from chapter XX of the original (Interest, Credit Expansion, and the Trade Cycle).

Chapter 7 integrates the previous considerations into a discussion of the market economy, presented as the foremost social body. Entrepreneurs activate it but consumers reign supreme, granting entrepreneurial profit to those who best anticipate the future state of affairs. The formation of prices is discussed, including that of human services (wages). It corresponds roughly to chapters XIV (The Scope and Method of Catallactics), XV (The market), XVI (Prices), XXI (Work and Wages), XXIII (The Data of the Market) and XXIV (Harmony and Conflict of Interests) of the original work.

Chapter 8 covers the more political parts of Human Action. Starting with an analysis of human cooperation as an intrinsic feature of man in society, it presents the classical liberal views about the respective place of the individual and government, the meaning of laissez faire, and dispels usual misconceptions about the relationships between individualism, liberalism and religion. This chapter gathers passages from chapters VIII (Human Society), X (Exchange Within Society), XV (The market), XXIV (Harmony and Conflict of Interests) and XXVII to XXX of the original book, about the hampered market economy.

This selection does not include any excerpt from chapters XXII (The Nonhuman Original Factors of Production), XXXV et XXXVI, which form part five (Social cooperation without a market), XXXI to XXXVI which are part of part six (The hampered market economy) and XXXVII (The Nondescript Character of Economics).

This selection is obviously not intended for readers already familiar with Mises' work, who can only find in it flaws and omissions, but hopefully no misrepresentations or downright mistakes. Although I have tried to remain faithful to Mises' thought throughout this work, it is unavoidable that my own judgment be somehow reflected in the selection and arrangement of paragraphs.

My goal, however, is definitely not that this selection be used in lieu of the original book, but only as an introduction and as a kind of an appetizer in order to motivate people to read the full text and learn all there is to learn from it – and maybe more important, to unlearn what they were taught under the attractive but misleading caption of "economic science".

Gérard Dréan

The place of economics in the sciences

The scope of economics

There have never been any doubts and uncertainties about the scope of economic science. Ever since people have been eager for a systematic study of economics or political economy, all have agreed that it is the task of this branch of knowledge to investigate the market phenomena, that is, the determination of the mutual exchange ratios of the goods and services negotiated on markets, their origin in human action and their effects upon later action. [14,1]

The intricacy of a precise definition of the scope of economics does not stem from uncertainty with regard to the orbit of the phenomena to be investigated. It is due to the fact that the attempts to elucidate the phenomena concerned must go beyond the range of the market and of market transactions. In order to conceive the market fully one is forced to study the action of hypothetical isolated individuals on one hand and to contrast the market system with an imaginary socialist commonwealth on the other hand. In studying interpersonal exchange one cannot avoid dealing with autistic exchange. But then it is no longer possible to define neatly the boundaries between the kind of action which is the proper field of economic science in the narrower sense, and other action. Economics widens its horizon and turns into a general science of all and every human action, into praxeology. The question emerges of how to distinguish precisely, within the broader field of general praxeology, a narrower orbit of specifically economic problems. [14,1]

The general theory of choice and preference goes far beyond the horizon which encompassed the scope of economic problems as circumscribed by the economists from Cantillon, Hume, and Adam Smith down to John Stuart Mill. It is much more than merely a theory of the "economic side" of human endeavors and of man's striving for commodities and an improvement in his material well-being. It is the science of every kind of human action. Choosing determines all human decisions. In making his choice man chooses not only between various material things and services. All human values are offered for option. All ends and all means, both material and ideal issues, the sublime and the base, the noble and the ignoble, are ranged in a single row and subjected to a decision which picks out one thing and sets aside another. Nothing that men aim at or want to avoid remains outside of this arrangement into a unique scale of gradation and preference. [0,1]

Man's freedom to choose and to act is restricted in a threefold way. There are first the physical laws to whose unfeeling absoluteness man must adjust his conduct if he wants to live. There are second the individual's innate constitutional characteristics and dispositions and the operation of environmental factors; we know that they influence both the choice of the ends and that of the means, although our cognizance of the mode of their operation is rather vague. There is finally the regularity of phenomena with regard to the interconnectedness of means and ends, viz, the praxeological law as distinct from the physical and from the physiological law. [39,3]

The elucidation and the categorial and formal examination of this third class of laws of the universe is the subject matter of praxeology and its hitherto best-developed branch, economics. The body of economic knowledge is an essential element in the structure of human civilization; it is the foundation upon which modern industrialism and all the moral, intellectual, technological, and therapeutical achievements of the last centuries have been built. [39,3]

The scope of praxeology, the general theory of human action, can be precisely defined and circumscribed. The specifically economic problems, the problems of economic action in the narrower sense, can only by and large be disengaged from the comprehensive body of praxeological theory. [14,1]

The abortive attempts to solve this problem of a precise delimitation of the scope of catallactics[4] have chosen as a criterion either the motives causing action or the goals which action aims at. But the variety and manifoldness of the motives instigating a man's action are without relevance for a comprehensive study of acting. Every action is motivated by the urge to remove a felt uneasiness. It does not matter for the science of action how people qualify this uneasiness from a physiological, psychological, or ethical point of view. It is the task of economics to deal with all commodity prices as they are really asked and paid in market transactions. It must not restrict its investigations to the study of those prices which result or are likely to result from a conduct displaying attitudes to which psychology, ethics, or any other way of looking at human behavior would attach a definite label. The classification of actions according to their various motives may be momentous for psychology and may provide a yardstick for a moral evaluation; for economics it is inconsequential. [14,1]

Essentially the same is valid with regard to the endeavors to restrict the scope of economics to those actions which aim at supplying people with tangible material things of the external universe. Strictly speaking, people do not long for tangible goods as such, but for the services which these goods are fitted to render them. They want to attain the increment in well-being which these services are able to convey. But if this is so, it is not permissible to except from the orbit of "economic" action those actions which remove uneasiness directly without the interposition of any tangible and visible things. The advice of a doctor, the instruction of a teacher, the recital of an artist, and other personal services are no less an object of economic studies than the architect's plans for the construction of a building, the scientist's formula for the production of a chemi-

4 Catallactics: the theory of market exchanges ("The subject matter of catallactics is all market phenomena with all their roots, ramifications, and consequences." [14, 1]) Mises uses that word as practically equivalent to "economics".

cal compound, and the author's contribution to the publishing of a book. [14,1]

The physical sciences and the human sciences

The experience with which the sciences of human action have to deal is always an experience of complex phenomena. No laboratory experiments can be performed with regard to human action. We are never in a position to observe the change in one element only, all other conditions of the event remaining unchanged. Historical experience as an experience of complex phenomena does not provide us with facts in the sense in which the natural sciences employ this term to signify isolated events tested in experiments. The information conveyed by historical experience cannot be used as building material for the construction of theories and the prediction of future events. Every historical experience is open to various interpretations, and is in fact interpreted in different ways. [2,1]

The fullness of reality can be mentally mastered only by a mind resorting both to the conception of praxeology and to the understanding of history; and the latter requires command of the teachings of the natural sciences. Cognition and prediction are provided by the totality of knowledge. What the various single branches of science offer is always fragmentary; it must be complemented by the results of all the other branches. From the point of view of acting man the specialization of knowledge and its breaking up into the various sciences is merely a device of the division of labor. In the same way in which the consumer utilizes the products of various branches of production, the actor must base his decisions on knowledge brought about by various branches of thought and investigation. [23,1]

In the realm of physical and chemical events there exist (or, at least, it is generally assumed that there exist) constant relations between magnitudes, and man is capable of discovering these constants with a reasonable degree of precision by means of laboratory experiments. No such constant relations exist in the field of human action outside of physical and chemical technology and therapeutics. There are, in the field of economics, no constant relations, and consequently no measurement is possible. If a statistician determines that a rise of 10 per cent in the supply of potatoes in Atlantis at a definite time was followed by a fall of 8 per cent in the price, he does not establish anything about what happened or may happen with a change in the supply of potatoes in another country or at another time. He has not "measured" the "elasticity of demand" of potatoes. He has established a unique and individual historical fact. No intelligent man can doubt that the behavior of men with regard to potatoes, and every other commodity is variable. Different individuals value the same things in a different way, and valuations change with the same individuals with changing conditions. [2,8]

The impracticability of measurement is not due to the lack of technical methods for the establishment of measure. It is due to the absence of constant relations. If it were only caused by technical insufficiency, at least an approximate estimation would be possible in some cases. But the main fact is that there are no constant relations. Economics is not, as ignorant positivists repeat again and again, backward because it is not "quantitative." It is not quantitative and does not measure because there are no constants. [2,8]

Technology can tell us how thick a steel plate must be in order not to be pierced by a bullet fired at a distance of 300 yards from a Winchester rifle. It can thus answer the question why a man who took shelter behind a steel plate of a known thickness was hurt or not hurt by a shot fired. History is at a loss to explain with the same assurance why there was a rise in the price of milk of 10 per cent or why President Roosevelt defeated Governor Dewey in the election of 1944 or why France was from 1870 to 1940 under a republican constitution. [2,8]

In physics we are faced with changes occurring in various sense phenomena. We discover a regularity in the sequence of these changes and these observations lead us to the construction of a science of physics. We know nothing about the ultimate forces actuating these changes. They are for the searching mind ultimately given and defy any further analysis. What we know from observation is the regular concatenation of various observable entities and attributes. It is this mutual interdependence of data that the physicist describes in differential equations. [16,5]

In praxeology the first fact we know is that men are purposively intent upon bringing about some changes. It is this knowledge that integrates the subject matter of praxeology and differentiates it from the subject matter of the natural sciences. We know the forces behind the changes, and this aprioristic knowledge leads us to a cognition of the praxeological processes. The physicist does not know what electricity "is." He knows only phenomena attributed to something called electricity. But the economist knows what actuates the market process. It is only thanks to this knowledge that he is in a position to distinguish market phenomena from other phenomena and to describe the market process. [16,5]

In speaking of the laws of nature we have in mind the fact that there prevails an inexorable interconnectedness of physical and biological phenomena and that acting man must submit to this regularity if he wants to succeed. In speaking of the laws of human action we refer to the fact that such an inexorable interconnectedness of phenomena is present also in the field of human action as such and that acting man must recognize this regularity too if he wants to succeed. The reality of the laws of praxeology is revealed to man by the same signs that reveal the reality of natural law, namely, the fact that his power to attain chosen ends is restricted and conditioned. In the absence of laws man would either be omnipotent and would never feel any uneasiness which he could not remove instantly and totally, or he could not act at all. [30,1]

These laws of the universe must not be confused with the man-made laws of the country and with man-made moral precepts. The laws of the universe about which physics, biology, and praxeology provide knowledge are independent of the human will, they are primary ontological facts rigidly restricting man's power to act. The moral precepts and the laws of the country are means by which men seek to attain certain ends. Whether or not these ends can really be attained this way depends on the laws of the universe. The man-made laws are suitable if they are fit to attain these ends and contrary to purpose if they are not. They are open to examination from the point of view of their suitableness or unsuitableness. With regard to the laws of the universe any doubt of their suitableness is supererogatory and vain. They are what they are and take care of themselves. Their violation penalizes itself. But the man-made laws need to be enforced by special sanctions. [30,1]

Only the insane venture to disregard physical and biological laws. But it is quite common to disdain praxeological laws. Rulers do not like to admit that their power is restricted by any laws other than those of physics and biology. They never ascribe their failures and frustrations to the violation of economic law. [30,1]

Praxeology

The scope of praxeology is the explication of the category of human action. All that is needed for the deduction of all praxeological theorems is knowledge of the essence of human action. It is a knowledge that is our own because we are men; no being of human descent that pathological conditions have not reduced to a merely vegetative existence lacks it. No special experience is needed in order to comprehend these theorems, and no experience, however rich, could disclose them to a being who did not know a priori what human action is. The only way to a cognition of these theorems is logical analysis of our inherent knowledge of the category of action. We must bethink ourselves and reflect upon the structure of human action. Like logic and mathematics, praxeological knowledge is in us; it does not come from without. [2,10]

Praxeology deals with human action as such in a general and universal way. It deals neither with the particular conditions of the environment in which man acts nor with the concrete content of the valuations which direct his actions. For praxeology, data are the bodily and psychological features of the acting men, their desires and value judgments, and the theories, doctrines, and ideologies they develop in order to adjust themselves purposively to the conditions of their environment and thus to attain the ends they are aiming at. These data, although permanent in their structure and strictly determined by the laws controlling the order of the universe, are perpetually fluctuating and varying; they change from instant to instant. [23,1]

The field of our science is human action, not the psychological events which result in an action. It is precisely this which distinguishes the general theory of human action, praxeology, from psychology. The theme of psychology is the internal events that result or can result in a definite action. The theme of praxeology is action as such. This also settles the relation of praxeology to the psychoanalytical concept of the subconscious. Psychoanalysis too is psychology and does not investigate action but the forces and factors that impel a man toward a definite action. The psychoanalytical subconscious is a psychological and not a praxeological category. Whether an action stems from clear deliberation, or from forgotten memories and suppressed desires which from submerged regions, as it were, direct the will, does not influence the nature of the action. The murderer whom a subconscious urge (the Id) drives toward his crime and the neurotic whose aberrant behavior seems to be simply meaningless to an untrained observer both act; they like anybody else are aiming at certain ends. [1,1]

Since time immemorial men have been eager to know the prime mover, the cause of all being and of all change, the ultimate substance from which everything stems and which is the cause of itself. Science is more modest. It is aware of the limits of the human mind and of the human search for knowledge. It aims at tracing back every phenomenon to its cause. But it realizes that these endeavors must necessarily strike against insurmountable walls. There are phenomena which cannot be analyzed and traced back to other phenomena. They are the ultimate given. The progress of scientific research may succeed in demonstrating that something previously considered as an ultimate given can be reduced to components. But there will always be some irreducible and unanalyzable phenomena, some ultimate given. [1,3]

The teachings of praxeology and economics are valid for every human action without regard to its underlying motives, causes, and goals. The ultimate judgments of value and the ultimate ends of human action are given for any kind of scientific inquiry; they are not open to any further analysis. Praxeology deals with the ways and means chosen for the attainment of such ultimate ends. Its object is means, not ends. [1,4]

In this sense we speak of the subjectivism of the general science of human action. It takes the ultimate ends chosen by acting man as data, it is entirely neutral with regard to them, and it refrains from passing any value judgments. The only standard which it applies is whether or not the means chosen are fit for the attainment of the ends aimed at. At the same time it is in this subjectivism that the objectivity of our science lies. Because it is subjectivistic and takes the value judgments of acting man as ultimate data not open to any further critical examination, it is itself above all strife of parties and factions, it is indifferent to the conflicts of all schools of dogmatism and ethical doctrines, it is free from valuations and preconceived ideas and judgments, it is universally valid and absolutely and plainly human. [1,4]

It does not matter for man whether or not beyond the sphere accessible to the human mind there are other spheres in which there is something categorially different from human thinking and acting. No knowledge from such spheres penetrates to the human mind. It is idle to ask whether things-in-themselves are different from what they appear to us, and whether there are worlds which we cannot divine and ideas which we cannot comprehend. These are problems beyond the scope of human cognition. Human knowledge is conditioned by the structure of the human mind. [2,2]

Thus praxeology is human in a double sense. It is human because it claims for its theorems, within the sphere precisely defined in the underlying assumptions, universal validity for all human action. It is human moreover because it deals only with human action and does not aspire to know anything about nonhuman – whether subhuman or superhuman – action. [2,2]

Human reason

The categories of human thought and action are neither arbitrary products of the human mind nor conventions. They are not outside of the universe and of the course of cosmic events. They are biological facts and have a definite function in life and reality. They are instruments in man's struggle for existence and in his endeavors to adjust himself as much as possible to the real state of the universe and to remove uneasiness as much as it is in his power to do so. They are therefore appropriate to the structure of the external world and reflect properties of the world and of reality. They work, and are in this sense true and valid. [3,4]

Reason is man's particular and characteristic feature. There is no need for praxeology to raise the question whether reason is a suitable tool for the cognition of ultimate and absolute truth. It deals with reason only as far as it enables man to act. [9,1]

Reason's biological function is to preserve and to promote life and to postpone its extinction as long as possible. Thinking and acting are not contrary to nature; they are, rather, the foremost features of man's nature. The most appropriate description of man as differentiated from nonhuman beings is: a being purposively struggling against the forces adverse to his life. [39,1]

Hence all talk about the primacy of irrational elements is vain. Within the universe the existence of which our reason cannot explain, analyze, or conceive, there is a narrow field left within which man is capable of removing uneasiness to some extent. This is the realm of reason and rationality, of science and purposive action. [39,1]

It is vain to object that life and reality are not logical. Life and reality are neither logical nor illogical; they are simply given. But logic is the only tool available to man for the comprehension of both. [2,10]

Judicious rationalists do not pretend that human reason can ever make man omniscient. They are fully aware of the fact that, however knowledge may increase, there will always remain things ultimately given and not liable to any further elucidation. But, they say, as far as man is able to attain cognition, he must rely upon reason. The ultimate given is the irrational. The knowable is, as far as it is known already, necessarily rational. There is neither an irrational mode of cognition nor a science of irrationality. [3,6]

It is impossible to demonstrate the validity of the a priori foundations of logic and praxeology without referring to these foundations themselves. Reason is an ultimate given and cannot be analyzed or questioned by itself. The very existence of human reason is a nonrational fact. The only statement that can be predicated with regard to reason is that it is the mark that distinguishes man from animals and has brought about everything that is specifically human. [3,6]

If there had been races which had developed a different logical structure of the mind, they would have failed in the use of reason as an aid in the struggle for existence. The only means for survival that could have protected them against extermination would have been their instinctive reactions. Natural selection would have eliminated those specimens of such races that tried to employ reasoning for the direction of their behavior. Those individuals alone would have survived that relied upon instincts only. This means that only those would have had a chance to survive that did not rise above the mental level of animals. [3,4]

It is a poor makeshift to dispose of a theory by referring to its historical background, to the "spirit" of its time, to the material conditions of the country of its origin, and to any personal qualities of its authors. A theory is subject to the tribunal of reason only. The yardstick to be applied is always the yardstick of reason. A theory is either correct or incorrect. It may happen that the present state of our knowledge does not allow a decision with regard to its correctness or incorrectness. But a theory can never be valid for a bourgeois or an American if it is invalid for a proletarian or a Chinese. [3,6]

Economics as a discipline

The procedure of economics

Praxeology – and consequently economics too – is a deductive system. It draws its strength from the starting point of its deductions, from the category of action. No economic theorem can be considered sound that is not solidly fastened upon this foundation by an irrefutable chain of reasoning. A statement proclaimed without such a connection is arbitrary and floats in midair. It is impossible to deal with a special segment of economics if one does not encase it in a complete system of action. [2,10]

Economics does not allow of any breaking up into special branches. It invariably deals with the interconnectedness of all the phenomena of action. The catallactic problems cannot become visible if one deals with each branch of production separately. It is impossible to study labor and wages without studying implicitly commodity prices, interest rates, profit and loss, money and credit, and all the other major problems. The real problems of the determination of wage rates cannot even be touched in a course on labor. There are no such things as "economics of labor" or "economics of agriculture." There is only one coherent body of economics. [38,4]

What assigns economics its peculiar and unique position in the orbit both of pure knowledge and of the practical utilization of knowledge is the fact that its particular theorems are not open to any verification or falsification on the ground of experience. Of course, a measure suggested by sound economic reasoning results in producing the effects aimed at, and

a measure suggested by faulty economic reasoning fails to produce the ends sought. But such experience is always still historical experience, i.e., the experience of complex phenomena. It
can never, as has been pointed out, prove or disprove any particular theorem. The application of spurious economic theorems results in undesired consequences. But these effects never
have that undisputable power of conviction which the experimental facts in the field of the natural sciences provide. The ultimate yardstick of an economic theorem's correctness or incorrectness is solely reason unaided by experience. [37,1]

In the field of praxeological knowledge neither success
nor failure speaks a distinct language audible to everybody. The
experience derived exclusively from complex phenomena does
not bar escape into interpretations based on wishful thinking.
The naive man's propensity to ascribe omnipotence to his
thoughts, however confused and contradictory, is never manifestly and unambiguously falsified by experience. The economist can never refute the economic cranks and quacks in the way
in which the doctor refutes the medicine man and the char-
latan. History speaks only to those people who know how to
interpret it on the ground of correct theories. [37,1]

Even the most faithful examination of a chapter of economic history, though it be the history of the most recent
period of the past, is no substitute for economic thinking. Economics, like logic and mathematics, is a display of abstract
reasoning. Economics can never be experimental and empirical. The economist does not need an expensive apparatus for
the conduct of his studies. What he needs is the power to think
clearly and to discern in the wilderness of events what is essential from what is merely accidental. [38,1]

Man is not infallible. He searches for truth – that is, for
the most adequate comprehension of reality as far as the structure of his mind and reason makes it accessible to him. Man
can never become omniscient. He can never be absolutely certain that his inquiries were not misled and that what he considers as certain truth is not error. All that man can do is to
submit all his theories again and again to the most critical reex-
amination. This means for the economist to trace back all theorems to their unquestionable and certain ultimate basis, the

category of human action, and to test by the most careful scrutiny all assumptions and inferences leading from this basis to the theorem under examination. It cannot be contended that this procedure is a guarantee against error. But it is undoubtedly the most effective method of avoiding error. [2,10]

The method of imaginary constructions

The specific method of economics is the method of imaginary constructions. [14,2]

An imaginary construction is a conceptual image of a sequence of events logically evolved from the elements of action employed in its formation. It is a product of deduction, ultimately derived from the fundamental category of action, the act of preferring and setting aside. In designing such an imaginary construction the economist is not concerned with the question of whether or not it depicts the conditions of reality which he wants to analyze. Nor does he bother about the question of whether or not such a system as his imaginary construction posits could be conceived as really existent and in operation. Even imaginary constructions which are inconceivable, self-contradictory, or unrealizable can render useful, even indispensable services in the comprehension of reality, provided the economist knows how to use them properly. [14,2]

The method of imaginary constructions is justified by its success. Praxeology cannot, like the natural sciences, base its teachings upon laboratory experiments and sensory perception of external objects. It had to develop methods entirely different from those of physics and biology. It would be a serious blunder to look for analogies to the imaginary constructions in the field of the natural sciences. The imaginary constructions of praxeology can never be confronted with any experience of things external and can never be appraised from the point of view of such experience. Their function is to serve man in a scrutiny which cannot rely upon his senses. In confronting the imaginary constructions with reality we cannot raise the question of whether they correspond to experience and depict adequately the empirical data. We must ask whether the assumptions of our construction are identical with the conditions of those actions which we want to conceive. [14,2]

The main formula for designing of imaginary constructions is to abstract from the operation of some conditions present in actual action. Then we are in a position to grasp the hypothetical consequences of the absence of these conditions and to conceive the effects of their existence. Thus we conceive the category of action by constructing the image of a state in which there is no action, either because the individual is fully contented and does not feel any uneasiness or because he does not know any procedure from which an improvement in his well-being (state of satisfaction) could be expected. [14,2]

The states of rest

The only method of dealing with the problem of action is to conceive that action ultimately aims at bringing about a state of affairs in which there is no longer any action, whether because all uneasiness has been removed or because any further removal of felt uneasiness is out of the question. Action thus tends toward a state of rest, absence of action. [14,5]

The theory of prices accordingly analyzes interpersonal exchange from this aspect. People keep on exchanging on the market until no further exchange is possible because no party expects any further improvement of its own conditions from a new act of exchange. The potential buyers consider the prices asked by the potential sellers unsatisfactory, and vice versa. No more transactions take place. A state of rest emerges. This state of rest, which we may call the plain state of rest, is not an imaginary construction. It comes to pass again and again. When the stock market closes, the brokers have carried out all orders which could be executed at the market price. Only those potential sellers and buyers who consider the market price too low or too high respectively have not sold or bought. The same is valid with regard to all transactions. The whole market economy is a big exchange or market place, as it were. At any instant all those transactions take place which the parties are ready to enter into at the realizable price. New sales can be effected only when the valuations of at least one of the parties have changed. [14,5]

In dealing with the plain state of rest we look only at what is going on right now. We restrict our attention to what has happened momentarily and disregard what will happen later, in the next instant or tomorrow or later. We are dealing only with prices really paid in sales, i.e., with the prices of the immediate past. We do not ask whether or not future prices will equal these prices. [14,5]

But now we go a step further. We pay attention to factors which are bound to bring about a tendency toward price changes. We try to find out to what goal this tendency must lead before all its driving force is exhausted and a new state of rest emerges. The price corresponding to this future state of rest was called the natural price by older economists; nowadays the term static price is often used. In order to avoid misleading associations it is more expedient to call it the final price and accordingly to speak of the final state of rest. This final state of rest is an imaginary construction, not a description of reality. For the final state of rest will never be attained. New disturbing factors will emerge before it will be realized. What makes it necessary to take recourse to this imaginary construction is the fact that the market at every instant is moving toward a final state of rest. Every later new instant can create new facts altering this final state of rest. But the market is always disquieted by a striving after a definite final state of rest. [14,5]

The market price is a real phenomenon; it is the exchange ratio which was actual in business transacted. The final price is a hypothetical price. The market prices are historical facts and we are therefore in a position to note them with numerical exactitude in dollars and cents. The final price can only be defined by defining the conditions required for its emergence. No definite numerical value in monetary terms or in quantities of other goods can be attributed to it. It will never appear on the market. The market price can never coincide with the final price coordinated to the instant in which this market structure is actual. [14,5]

The phenomenon with which we have to cope is the fact that changes in the factors which determine the formation of prices do not produce all their effects at once. A span of time must elapse before all their effects are exhausted. Between the appearance of a new datum and the perfect adjustment of the market to it some time must pass. (And, of course, while this period of time elapses, other new data appear.) In dealing with the effects of any change in the factors operating on the market, we must never forget that we are dealing with events taking place in succession, with a series of effects succeeding one another. We are not in a position to know in advance how much time will have to elapse. But we know for certain that some time must elapse, although this period may sometimes be so small that it hardly plays any role in practical life. [14,5]

The imaginary construction of the evenly rotating economy

The evenly rotating economy is a fictitious system in which the market prices of all goods and services coincide with the final prices. There are in its frame no price changes whatever; there is perfect price stability. The same market transactions are repeated again and again. The goods of the higher orders pass in the same quantities through the same stages of processing until ultimately the produced consumers' goods come into the hands of the consumers and are consumed. No changes in the market data occur. Today does not differ from yesterday and tomorrow will not differ from today. The system is in perpetual flux, but it remains always at the same spot. [14,5]

The essence of this imaginary construction is the elimination of the lapse of time and of the perpetual change in the market phenomena. The notion of any change with regard to supply and demand is incompatible with this construction. Only such changes as do not affect the configuration of the price-determining factors can be considered in its frame. [14,5]

In reality there is never such a thing as an evenly rotating economic system. However, in order to analyze the problems of change in the data and of unevenly and irregularly varying movement, we must confront them with a fictitious state in which both are hypothetically eliminated. [14,5]

Action is change, and change is in the temporal sequence. But in the evenly rotating economy change and succession of events are eliminated. Action is to make choices and to cope with an uncertain future. But in the evenly rotating economy there is no choosing and the future is not uncertain as it does not differ from the present known state. Such a rigid system is not peopled with living men making choices and liable to error; it is a world of soulless unthinking automatons; it is not a human society, it is an ant hill. [14,5]

These insoluble contradictions, however, do not affect the service which this imaginary construction renders for the only problems for whose treatment it is both appropriate and indispensable: the problem of the relation between the prices of products and those of the factors required for their production, and the implied problems of entrepreneurship and of profit and loss. [14,5]

In order to grasp the function of entrepreneurship and the meaning of profit and loss, we construct a system from which they are absent. This image is merely a tool for our thinking. It is not the description of a possible and realizable state of affairs. It is even out of the question to carry the imaginary construction of an evenly rotating system to its ultimate logical consequences. For it is impossible to eliminate the entrepreneur from the picture of a market economy. The various complementary factors of production cannot come together spontaneously. They need to be combined by the purposive efforts of men aiming at certain ends and motivated by the urge to improve their state of satisfaction. In eliminating the entrepreneur one eliminates the driving force of the whole market system. [14,5]

Then there is a second deficiency. In the imaginary construction of an evenly rotating economy, indirect exchange and the use of money are tacitly implied. But what kind of money can that be? In a system without change in which there is no uncertainty whatever about the future, nobody needs to hold cash. Every individual knows precisely what amount of money he will need at any future date. He is therefore in a position to lend all the funds he receives in such a way that the loans fall due on the date he will need them. [14,5]

It has been pointed out already that in the imaginary construction of an evenly rotating economy the very notion of money vanishes into an unsubstantial calculation process, self-contradictory and devoid of any meaning. It is impossible to assign any function to indirect exchange, media of exchange, and money within an imaginary construction the characteristic mark of which is unchangeability and rigidity of conditions. [17,5]

The imaginary construction of an evenly rotating system is a limiting notion. In its frame there is in fact no longer any action. Automatic reaction is substituted for the conscious striving of thinking man after the removal of uneasiness. We can employ this problematic imaginary construction only if we never forget what purposes it is designed to serve. We want first of all to analyze the tendency, prevailing in every action, toward the establishment of an evenly rotating economy; in doing so, we must always take into account that this tendency can never attain its goal in a universe not perfectly rigid and immutable, that is, in a universe which is living and not dead. Secondly, we need to comprehend in what respects the conditions of a living world in which there is action differ from those of a rigid world. This we can discover only by the *argumentum a contrario* provided by the image of a rigid economy. Thus we are led to the insight that dealing with the uncertain conditions of the unknown future – that is, speculation – is inherent in every action, and that profit and loss are necessary features of acting which cannot be conjured away by any wishful thinking. The procedures adopted by those economists who are fully aware of these fundamental cognitions may be called the logical method of economics as contrasted with the technique of the mathematical method. [14,5]

The mathematical economists disregard dealing with the actions which, under the imaginary and unrealizable assumption that no further new data will emerge, are supposed to bring about the evenly rotating economy. They do not notice the individual speculator who aims not at the establishment of the evenly rotating economy but at profiting from an action which adjusts the conduct of affairs better to the attainment of the ends sought by acting, the best possible removal of uneasiness. They stress exclusively the imaginary state of equilibrium which the whole complex of all such actions would attain in the absence of any further change in the data. They describe this imaginary equilibrium by sets of simultaneous differential equations. They fail to recognize that the state of affairs they are dealing with is a state in which there is no longer any action but only a succession of events provoked by a mystical prime mover. They devote all their efforts to describing, in mathematical symbols, various "equilibria," that is, states of rest and the absence of action. They deal with equilibrium as if it were a real entity and not a limiting notion, a mere mental tool. What they are doing is vain playing with mathematical symbols, a pastime not suited to convey any knowledge. [14,5]

The imaginary construction of the stationary economy

The stationary economy is an economy in which the wealth and income of the individuals remain unchanged. With this image changes are compatible which would be incompatible with the construction of the evenly rotating economy. Population figures may rise or drop provided that they are accompanied by a corresponding rise or drop in the sum of wealth and income. The demand for some commodities may change; but these changes must occur so slowly that the transfer of capital from those branches of production which are to be restricted in accordance with them into those to be expanded can be effected by not replacing equipment used up in the shrinking branches and instead investing in the expanding ones. [14,6]

The imaginary construction of a stationary economy leads to two further imaginary constructions: the progressing (expanding) economy and the retrogressing (shrinking) economy. In the former the per capita quota of wealth and income of the individuals and the population figure tend toward a higher numerical value, in the latter toward a lower numerical value. [14,6]

In the stationary economy the total sum of all profits and of all losses is zero. In the progressing economy the total amount of profits exceeds the total amount of losses. In the retrogressing economy the total amount of profits is smaller than the total amount of losses. [14,6]

The precariousness of these three imaginary constructions is to be seen in the fact that they imply the possibility of the measurement of wealth and income. As such measurements cannot be made and are not even conceivable, it is out of the question to apply them for a rigorous classification of the conditions of reality. [14,6]

Logical economics versus mathematical economics

The problems of prices and costs have been treated also with mathematical methods. There have even been economists who held that the only appropriate method of dealing with economic problems is the mathematical method and who derided the logical economists as "literary" economists[5]. [16,5]

If this antagonism between the logical and the mathematical economists were merely a disagreement concerning the most adequate procedure to be applied in the study of economics, it would be superfluous to pay attention to it. The better method would prove its preeminence by bringing about better results. It may also be that different varieties of procedure are necessary for the solution of different problems and that for some of them one method is more useful than the other. [16,5]

However, this is not a dispute about heuristic questions, but a controversy concerning the foundations of economics. The mathematical method must be rejected not only on account of its barrenness. It is an entirely vicious method, starting from false assumptions and leading to fallacious inferences.

---

5 This was written in the forties. It is interesting that Mises is using the past tense ("there have even been economists who held..."). He would be disappointed that they now seem to be a majority!

Its syllogisms are not only sterile; they divert the mind from the study of the real problems and distort the relations between the various phenomena. [16,5]

Experience of economic history is always experience of complex phenomena. It can never convey knowledge of the kind the experimenter abstracts from a laboratory experiment. Statistics is a method for the presentation of historical facts concerning prices and other relevant data of human action. It is not economics and cannot produce economic theorems and theories. The statistics of prices is economic history. The insight that, ceteris paribus, an increase in demand must result in an increase in prices is not derived from experience. Nobody ever was or ever will be in a position to observe a change in one of the market data ceteris paribus. There is no such thing as quantitative economics. All economic quantities we know about are data of economic history. No reasonable man can contend that the relation between price and supply is in general, or in respect of certain commodities, constant. We know, on the contrary, that external phenomena affect different people in different ways, that the reactions of the same people to the same external events vary, and that it is not possible to assign individuals to classes of men reacting in the same way. [16,5]

The second field treated by mathematical economists is that of the relation of prices and costs. In dealing with these problems the mathematical economists disregard the operation of the market process and moreover pretend to abstract from the use of money inherent in all economic calculations. However, as they speak of prices and costs in general and confront prices and costs, they tacitly imply the existence and the use of money. Prices are always money prices, and costs cannot be taken into account in economic calculation if not expressed in terms of money. If one does not resort to terms of money, costs are expressed in complex quantities of diverse goods and services to be expended for the procurement of a product. [16,5]

That the seller values the goods he gives away less than those he receives in exchange for them, that the seller and the buyer disagree with regard to the subjective valuation of the two goods exchanged, and that an entrepreneur embarks upon a project only if he expected to receive for the product goods that he values higher than those expended in their production, all this we know already on the ground of praxeological comprehension. It is this aprioristic knowledge that enables us to anticipate the conduct of an entrepreneur who is in a position to resort to economic calculation. But the mathematical economist deludes himself when he pretends to treat these problems in a more general way by omitting any reference to terms of money. [16,5]

It cannot be denied that all investigations concerning the relation of prices and costs presuppose both the use of money and the market process. But the mathematical economists shut their eyes to this obvious fact. They formulate equations and draw curves which are supposed to describe reality. In fact they describe only a hypothetical and unrealizable state of affairs, in no way similar to the catallactic problems in question. They substitute algebraic symbols for the determinate terms of money as used in economic calculation and believe that this procedure renders their reasoning more scientific. They strongly impress the gullible layman. In fact they only confuse and muddle things which are satisfactorily dealt with in textbooks of commercial arithmetic and accountancy. [16,5]

The deliberations which result in the formulation of an equation are necessarily of a nonmathematical character. The formulation of the equation is the consummation of our knowledge; it does not directly enlarge our knowledge. Yet, in mechanics the equation can render very important practical services. As there exist constant relations between various mechanical elements and as these relations can be ascertained by experiments, it becomes possible to use equations for the solution of definite technological problems. Our modern industrial civilization is mainly an accomplishment of this utilization of the differential equations of physics. No such constant relations exist, however, between economic elements. The equations formulated by mathematical economics remain a useless piece of mental gymnastics and would remain so even if they were to express much more than they really do. [16,5]

A sound economic deliberation must never forget these two fundamental principles of the theory of value: First, valuing that results in action always means preferring and setting aside; it never means equivalence or indifference. Second, there is no means of comparing the valuations of different individuals or the valuations of the same individuals at different instants other than by establishing whether or not they arrange the alternatives in question in the same order of preference. [16,5]

The fundamental deficiency implied in every quantitative approach to economic problems consists in the neglect of the fact that there are no constant relations between what are called economic dimensions. There is neither constancy nor continuity in the valuations and in the formation of exchange ratios between various commodities. Every new datum brings about a reshuffling of the whole price structure. [6,7]

Both the logical and the mathematical economists assert that human action ultimately aims at the establishment of such a state of equilibrium and would reach it if all further changes in data were to cease. But the logical economist knows much more than that. He shows how the activities of enterprising men, the promoters and speculators, eager to profit from discrepancies in the price structure, tend toward eradicating such discrepancies and thereby also toward blotting out the sources of entrepreneurial profit and loss. He shows how this process would finally result in the establishment of the evenly rotating economy. This is the task of economic theory. The mathematical description of various states of equilibrium is mere play. The problem is the analysis of the market process. [16,5]

Economics is not about goods and services, it is about the actions of living men. Its goal is not to dwell upon imaginary constructions such as equilibrium. These constructions are only tools of reasoning. The sole task of economics is analysis of the actions of men, is the analysis of processes. [16,5]

Judgments of value

In the course of social events there prevails a regularity of phenomena to which man must adjust his actions if he wishes to succeed. It is futile to approach social facts with the attitude of a censor who approves or disapproves from the point of view of quite arbitrary standards and subjective judgments of value. One must study the laws of human action and social cooperation as the physicist studies the laws of nature. [0,1]

What a man does is always aimed at an improvement of his own state of satisfaction. In this sense – and in no other – we are free to use the term selfishness and to emphasize that action is necessarily always selfish. Even an action directly aiming at the improvement of other people's conditions is selfish. The actor considers it as more satisfactory for himself to make other people eat than to eat himself. His uneasiness is caused by the awareness of the fact that other people are in want. [14,3]

The value judgments of an individual differentiate between what makes him more satisfied and what less. The value judgments a man pronounces about another man's satisfaction do not assert anything about this other man's satisfaction. They only assert what condition of this other man better satisfies the man who pronounces the judgment. The reformers searching for the maximum of general satisfaction have told us merely what state of other people's affairs would best suit themselves. [14,3]

Ethical doctrines are intent upon establishing scales of value according to which man should act but does not necessarily always act. They claim for themselves the vocation of telling right from wrong and of advising man concerning what he should aim at as the supreme good. They are normative disciplines aiming at the cognition of what ought to be. They are not neutral with regard to facts; they judge them from the point of view of freely adopted standards. [4,2]

This is not the attitude of praxeology and economics. They are fully aware of the fact that the ultimate ends of human action are not open to examination from any absolute standard. Ultimate ends are ultimately given, they are purely subjective, they differ with various people and with the same people at various moments in their lives. Praxeology and economics deal with the means for the attainment of ends chosen by the acting individuals. They do not express any opinion with regard to such problems as whether or not sybaritism is better than asceticism. They apply to the means only one yardstick, viz., whether or not they are suitable to attain the ends at which the acting individuals aim. [4,2]

Economics and the citizen

Economics must not be relegated to classrooms and statistical offices and must not be left to esoteric circles. It is the philosophy of human life and action and concerns everybody and everything. It is the pith of civilization and of man's human existence. [38,6]

All present-day political issues concern problems commonly called economic. All arguments advanced in contemporary discussion of social and public affairs deal with fundamental matters of praxeology and economics. Everybody's mind is preoccupied with economic doctrines. Philosophers and theologians seem to be more interested in economic problems than in those problems which earlier generations considered the subject matter of philosophy and theology. Novels and plays today treat all things human – including sex relations – from the angle of economic doctrines. Everybody thinks of economics whether he is aware of it or not. In joining a political party and in casting his ballot, the citizen implicitly takes a stand upon essential economic theories. [38,6]

There is no means by which anyone can evade his personal responsibility. Whoever neglects to examine to the best of his abilities all the problems involved voluntarily surrenders his birthright to a self-appointed elite of supermen. In such vital matters blind reliance upon "experts" and uncritical acceptance of popular catchwords and prejudices is tantamount to the abandonment of self-determination and to yielding to other people's domination. As conditions are today, nothing can be more important to every intelligent man than economics. His own fate and that of his progeny is at stake. [38,6]

If we look at all the theorems and theories guiding the conduct of certain individuals and groups as a coherent complex and try to arrange them as far as is feasible into a system, i.e., a comprehensive body of knowledge, we may speak of it as a world view. A world view is, as a theory, an interpretation of all things, and as a precept for action, an opinion concerning the best means for removing uneasiness as much as possible. A world view is thus, on the one hand, an explanation of all phenomena and, on the other hand, a technology, both these terms being taken in their broadest sense. Religion, metaphysics, and philosophy aim at providing a world view. They interpret the universe and they advise men how to act. [9,2]

The concept of an ideology is narrower than that of a world view. In speaking of ideology we have in view only human action and social cooperation and disregard the problems of metaphysics, religious dogma, the natural sciences, and the technologies derived from them. Ideology is the totality of our doctrines concerning individual conduct and social relations. Both, world view and ideology, go beyond the limits imposed upon a purely neutral and academic study of things as they are. They are not only scientific theories, but also doctrines about the ought, i.e., about the ultimate ends which man should aim at in his earthly concerns. [9,2]

Praxeology and economics are not qualified to deal with the transcendent and metaphysical aspects of any doctrine. But, on the other hand, no appeal to any religious or metaphysical dogmas and creeds can invalidate the theorems and theories concerning social cooperation as developed by logically correct praxeological reasoning. [9,2]

The main objective of praxeology and economics is to substitute consistent correct ideologies for the contradictory tenets of popular eclecticism. There is no other means of preventing social disintegration and of safeguarding the steady improvement of human conditions than those provided by reason. Men must try to think through all the problems involved up to the point beyond which a human mind cannot proceed farther. They must never acquiesce in any solutions conveyed by older generations, they must always question anew every theory and every theorem, they must never relax in their endeavors to brush away fallacies and to find the best possible cognition. They must fight error by unmasking spurious doctrines and by expounding truth. [9,2]

Economics as a profession

The development of a profession of economists is an offshoot of interventionism. The professional economist is the specialist who is instrumental in designing various measures of government interference with business. He is an expert in the field of economic legislation, which today invariably aims at hindering the operation of the market economy. [38,2]

The economist knows that a boom must result in a depression. But he does not and cannot know when the crisis will appear. This depends on the special conditions of each case. Many political events can influence the outcome. There are no rules according to which the duration of the boom or of the following depression can be computed. And even if such rules were available, they would be of no use to businessmen. What the individual businessman needs in order to avoid losses is knowledge about the date of the turning point at a time when other businessmen still believe that the crash is farther away than is really the case. Then his superior knowledge will give him the opportunity to arrange his own operations in such a way as to come out unharmed. But if the end of the boom could be calculated according to a formula, all businessmen would learn the date at the same time. Their endeavors to adjust their conduct of affairs to this information would immediately result in the appearance of all the phenomena of the depression. It would be too late for any of them to avoid being victimized. [38,3]

If it were possible to calculate the future state of the market, the future would not be uncertain. There would be neither entrepreneurial loss nor profit. What people expect from the economists is beyond the power of any mortal man. [38,3]

Entrepreneurial judgment cannot be bought on the market. The entrepreneurial idea that carries on and brings profit is precisely that idea which did not occur to the majority. It is not correct foresight as such that yields profits, but foresight better than that of the rest. The prize goes only to the dissenters, who do not let themselves be misled by the errors accepted by the multitude. What makes profits emerge is the provision for future needs for which others have neglected to make adequate provision. [38,3]

In fact reasonable businessmen are fully aware of the uncertainty of the future. They realize that the economists do not dispense any reliable information about things to come and that all that they provide is interpretation of statistical data referring to the past. For the capitalists and entrepreneurs the economists' opinions about the future count only as questionable conjectures. They are skeptical and not easily fooled. But as they quite correctly believe that it is useful to know all the data which could possibly have any relevance for their affairs, they subscribe to the newspapers and periodicals publishing the forecasts. Anxious not to neglect any source of information available, big business employs staffs of economists and statisticians. [38,3]

Business forecasting fails in the vain attempts to make the uncertainty of the future disappear and to deprive entrepreneurship of its inherent speculative character. But it renders some services in assembling and interpreting the available data about economic trends and developments of the recent past. [38,3]

Human action

The definition of human action

Economics deals with the real actions of real men. Its theorems refer neither to ideal nor to perfect men, neither to the phantom of a fabulous economic man (*homo oeconomicus*) nor to the statistical notion of an average man (*homme moyen*). Man with all his weaknesses and limitations, every man as he lives and acts, is the subject matter of catallactics. Every human action is a theme of praxeology. [23,4]

Human action is purposeful behavior. Or we may say: Action is will put into operation and transformed into an agency, is aiming at ends and goals, is the ego's meaningful response to stimuli and to the conditions of its environment, is a person's conscious adjustment to the state of the universe that determines his life. [1,1]

Action is not simply giving preference. Man also shows preference in situations in which things and events are un-avoidable or are believed to be so. Thus a man may prefer sun-shine to rain and may wish that the sun would dispel the clouds. He who only wishes and hopes does not interfere act-ively with the course of events and with the shaping of his own destiny. But acting man chooses, determines, and tries to reach an end. Of two things both of which he cannot have together he selects one and gives up the other. Action therefore always involves both taking and renunciation. [1,1]

To express wishes and hopes and to announce planned action may be forms of action in so far as they aim in them-selves at the realization of a certain purpose. But they must not be confused with the actions to which they refer. They are not identical with the actions they announce, recommend, or reject. Action is a real thing. What counts is a man's total behavior, and not his talk about planned but not realized acts. [1,1]

On the other hand action must be clearly distinguished from the application of labor. Action means the employment of means for the attainment of ends. As a rule one of the means employed is the acting man's labor. But this is not always the case. Under special conditions a word is all that is needed. He who gives orders or interdictions may act without any expenditure of labor. To talk or not to talk, to smile or to remain serious, may be action. To consume and to enjoy are no less action than to abstain from accessible consumption and enjoyment. [1,1]

Praxeology consequently does not distinguish between "active" or energetic and "passive" or indolent man. The vigorous man industriously striving for the improvement of his condition acts neither more nor less than the lethargic man who sluggishly takes things as they come. For to do nothing and to be idle are also action, they too determine the course of events. Wherever the conditions for human interference are present, man acts no matter whether he interferes or refrains from interfering. He who endures what he could change acts no less than he who interferes in order to attain another result. A man who abstains from influencing the operation of physiological and instinctive factors which he could influence also acts. Action is not only doing but no less omitting to do what possibly could be done. [1,1]

Methodological individualism

Praxeology deals with the actions of individual men. It is only in the further course of its inquiries that cognition of human cooperation is attained and social action is treated as a special case of the more universal category of human action as such. [2,4]

As a thinking and acting being man emerges from his prehuman existence already as a social being. The evolution of reason, language, and cooperation is the outcome of the same process; they were inseparably and necessarily linked together. But this process took place in individuals. It consisted in changes in the behavior of individuals. There is no other substance in which it occurred than the individuals. There is no substratum of society other than the actions of individuals. [2,4]

That there are nations, states, and churches, that there is social cooperation under the division of labor, becomes discernible only in the actions of certain individuals. Nobody ever perceived a nation without perceiving its members. In this sense one may say that a social collective comes into being through the actions of individuals. That does not mean that the individual is temporally antecedent. It merely means that definite actions of individuals constitute the collective. [2,4]

It is uncontested that in the sphere of human action social entities have real existence. Nobody ventures to deny that nations, states, municipalities, parties, religious communities, are real factors determining the course of human events. Methodological individualism, far from contesting the significance of such collective wholes, considers it as one of its main tasks to describe and to analyze their becoming and their disappearing, their changing structures, and their operation. And it chooses the only method fitted to solve this problem satisfactorily. [2,4]

First we must realize that all actions are performed by individuals. A collective operates always through the intermediary of one or several individuals whose actions are related to the collective as the secondary source. It is the meaning which the acting individuals and all those who are touched by their action attribute to an action, that determines its character. It is the meaning that marks one action as the action of an individual and another action as the action of the state or of the municipality. The hangman, not the state, executes a criminal. It is the meaning of those concerned that discerns in the hangman's action an action of the state. A group of armed men occupies a place. It is the meaning of those concerned which imputes this occupation not to the officers and soldiers on the spot, but to their nation. [2,4]

Goals

We call contentment or satisfaction that state of a human being which does not and cannot result in any action. Acting man is eager to substitute a more satisfactory state of affairs for a less satisfactory. His mind imagines conditions which suit him better, and his action aims at bringing about this desired state. The incentive that impels a man to act is always some uneasiness. A man perfectly content with the state of his affairs would have no incentive to change things. He would have neither wishes nor desires; he would be perfectly happy. He would not act; he would simply live free from care. [1,2]

But to make a man act, uneasiness and the image of a more satisfactory state alone are not sufficient. A third condition is required: the expectation that purposeful behavior has the power to remove or at least to alleviate the felt uneasiness. In the absence of this condition no action is feasible. Man must yield to the inevitable. He must submit to destiny. [1,2]

The ultimate goal of human action is always the satisfaction of the acting man's desire. There is no standard of greater or lesser satisfaction other than individual judgments of value, different for various people and for the same people at various times. What makes a man feel uneasy and less uneasy is established by him from the standard of his own will and judgment, from his personal and subjective valuation. Nobody is in a position to decree what should make a fellow man happier. [1,2]

To establish this fact does not refer in any way to the antitheses of egoism and altruism, of materialism and idealism, of individualism and collectivism, of atheism and religion. There are people whose only aim is to improve the condition of their own ego. There are other people with whom awareness of the troubles of their fellow men causes as much uneasiness as or even more uneasiness than their own wants. There are people who desire nothing else than the satisfaction of their appetites for sexual intercourse, food, drinks, fine homes, and other material things. But other men care more for the satisfactions commonly called "higher" and "ideal." There are individuals eager to adjust their actions to the requirements of social cooperation; there are, on the other hand, refractory people who defy the rules of social life. There are people for whom the ultimate goal of the earthly pilgrimage is the preparation for a life of bliss. There are other people who do not believe in the teachings of any religion and do not allow their actions to be influenced by them. [1,2]

Praxeology is indifferent to the ultimate goals of action. Its findings are valid for all kinds of action irrespective of the ends aimed at. It is a science of means, not of ends. It applies the term happiness in a purely formal sense. In the praxeological terminology the proposition: man's unique aim is to attain happiness, is tautological. It does not imply any statement about the state of affairs from which man expects happiness. [1,2]

Ends and means

The result sought by an action is called its end, goal, or aim. One uses these terms in ordinary speech also to signify intermediate ends, goals, or aims; these are points which acting man wants to attain only because he believes that he will reach his ultimate end, goal or aim in passing beyond them. Strictly speaking the end, goal, or aim of any action is always the relief from a felt uneasiness. [4,1]

A means is what serves to the attainment of any end, goal, or aim. Means are not in the given universe; in this universe there exist only things. A thing becomes a means when human reason plans to employ it for the attainment of some end and human action really employs it for this purpose. Thinking man sees the serviceableness of things, i.e., their ability to minister to his ends, and acting man makes them means. [4,1]

It is of primary importance to realize that parts of the external world become means only through the operation of the human mind and its offshoot, human action. External objects are as such only phenomena of the physical universe and the subject matter of the natural sciences. It is human meaning and action which transform them into means. [4,1]

Man is in a position to act because he has the ability to discover causal relations which determine change and becoming in the universe. Acting requires and presupposes the category of causality. Only a man who sees the world in the light of causality is fitted to act. In this sense we may say that causality is a category of action. The category means and ends presupposes the category cause and effect. In a world without causality and regularity of phenomena there would be no field for human reasoning and human action. Such a world would be a chaos in which man would be at a loss to find any orientation and guidance. Man is not even capable of imagining the conditions of such a chaotic universe. [1,5]

Praxeology does not deal with the external world. but with man's conduct with regard to it. Praxeological reality is not the physical universe, but man's conscious reaction to the given state of this universe. Economics is not about things and tangible material objects; it is about men, their meanings and actions. Goods, commodities, and wealth and all the other notions of conduct are not elements of nature; they are elements of human meaning and conduct. He who wants to deal with them must not look at the external world; he must search for them in the meaning of acting men. [4,1]

Praxeology and economics do not deal with human meaning and action as they should be or would be if all men were inspired by an absolutely valid philosophy and equipped with a perfect knowledge of technology. For such notions as absolute validity and omniscience there is no room in the frame of a science whose subject matter is erring man. An end is everything which men aim at. A means is everything which acting men consider as such. [4,1]

Means are necessarily always limited, i.e., scarce with regard to the services for which man wants to use them. If this were not the case, there would not be any action with regard to them. Where man is not restrained by the insufficient quantity of things available, there is no need for any action. [4,1]

Value

Value is the importance that acting man attaches to ultimate ends. Only to ultimate ends is primary and original value assigned. Means are valued derivatively according to their serviceableness in contributing to the attainment of ultimate ends. Their valuation is derived from the valuation of the respective ends. They are important for man only as far as they make it possible for him to attain some ends. [4,2]

Value is not intrinsic, it is not in things. It is within us; it is the way in which man reacts to the conditions of his environment. [4,2]

Neither is value in words and doctrines. It is reflected in human conduct. It is not what a man or groups of men say about value that counts, but how they act. The oratory of moralists and the pompousness of party programs are significant as such. But they influence the course of human events only as far as they really determine the actions of men. [4,2]

It is customary to say that acting man has a scale of wants or values in his mind when he arranges his actions. On the basis of such a scale he satisfies what is of higher value, i.e., his more urgent wants, and leaves unsatisfied what is of lower value, i.e., what is a less urgent want. There is no objection to such a presentation of the state of affairs. However, one must not forget that the scale of values or wants manifests itself only in the reality of action. These scales have no independent existence apart from the actual behavior of individuals. The only source from which our knowledge concerning these scales is derived is the observation of a man's actions. [4,2]

Notwithstanding all declarations to the contrary, the immense majority of men aim first of all at an improvement of the material conditions of well-being. They want more and better food, better homes and clothes, and a thousand other amenities. They strive after abundance and health. Taking these goals as given, applied physiology tries to determine what means are best suited to provide as much satisfaction as possible. It distinguishes, from this point of view, between man's "real" needs and imaginary and spurious appetites. It teaches people how they should act and what they should aim at as a means. [4,3]

The importance of such doctrines is obvious. From his point of view the physiologist is right in distinguishing between sensible action and action contrary to purpose. He is right in contrasting judicious methods of nourishment from unwise methods. He may condemn certain modes of behavior as absurd and opposed to "real" needs. However, such judgments are beside the point for a science dealing with the reality of human action. Not what a man should do, but what he does, counts for praxeology and economics. Hygiene may be right or wrong in calling alcohol and nicotine poisons. But economics must explain the prices of tobacco and liquor as they are, not as they would be under different conditions. [4,3]

There is no room left in the field of economics for a scale of needs different from the scale of values as reflected in man's actual behavior. Economics deals with real man, weak and subject to error as he is, not with ideal beings, omniscient and perfect as only gods could be. [4,3]

Some economists believe that it is the task of economics to establish how in the whole of society the greatest possible satisfaction of all people or of the greatest number could be attained. They do not realize that there is no method which would allow us to measure the state of satisfaction attained by various individuals. They misconstrue the character of judgments which are based on the comparison between various people's happiness. While expressing arbitrary value judgments, they believe themselves to be establishing facts. One may call it just to rob the rich in order to make presents to the poor. However, to call something fair or unfair is always a subjective value judgment and as such purely personal and not liable to any verification or falsification. Economics is not intent upon pronouncing value judgments. It aims at a cognition of the consequences of certain modes of acting. [14,3]

It is true that economics is a theoretical science and as such abstains from any judgment of value. It is not its task to tell people what ends they should aim at. It is a science of the means to be applied for the attainment of ends chosen, not, to be sure, a science of the choosing of ends. Ultimate decisions, the valuations and the choosing of ends, are beyond the scope of any science. Science never tells a man how he should act; it merely shows how a man must act if he wants to attain definite ends. [0,3]

While many people blame economics for its neutrality with regard to value judgments, other people blame it for its alleged indulgence in them. Some contend that economics must necessarily express judgments of value and is therefore not really scientific, as the criterion of science is its valuational indifference. Others maintain that good economics should be and could be impartial, and that only bad economists sin against this postulate. [39,2]

The semantic confusion in the discussion of the problems concerned is due to an inaccurate use of terms on the part of many economists. An economist investigates whether a measure a can bring about the result p for the attainment of which it is recommended, and finds that a does not result in p but in g. an effect which even the supporters of the measure a consider undesirable. If this economist states the outcome of his investigation by saying that a is a bad measure, he does not pronounce a judgment of value. He merely says that from the point of view of those aiming at the goal p, the measure a is inappropriate. [39,2]

From the same point of view praxeology and economics look upon the fundamental principle of human existence and social evolution, viz., that cooperation under the social division of labor is a more efficient way of acting than is the autarkic isolation of individuals. Praxeology and economics do not say that men should peacefully cooperate within the frame of societal bonds; they merely say that men must act this way if they want to make their actions more successful than otherwise. Compliance with the moral rules which the establishment, preservation, and intensification of social cooperation require is not seen as a sacrifice to a mythical entity, but as the recourse to the most efficient methods of action, as a price expended for the attainment of more highly valued returns. [39,2]

Economics does not assume or postulate that men aim only or first of all at what is called material well-being. Economics, as a branch of the more general theory of human action, deals with all human action, i.e., with man's purposive aiming at the attainment of ends chosen, whatever these ends may be. To apply the concept rational or irrational to the ultimate ends chosen is nonsensical. We may call irrational the ultimate given, viz., those things that our thinking can neither analyze nor reduce to other ultimately given things. Then every ultimate end chosen by any man is irrational. It is neither more nor less rational to aim at riches like Croesus than to aim at poverty like a Buddhist monk. [39,2]

Utility

Action sorts and grades; originally it knows only ordinal numbers, not cardinal numbers. But the external world to which acting man must adjust his conduct is a world of quantitative determinateness. In this world there exist quantitative relations between cause and effect. If it were otherwise, if definite things could render unlimited services, such things would never be scarce and could not be dealt with as means. [7,1]

Utility means in this context simply: causal relevance for the removal of felt uneasiness. Acting man believes that the services a thing can render are apt to improve his own well-being, and calls this the utility of the thing concerned. For praxeology the term utility is tantamount to importance attached to a thing on account of the belief that it can remove uneasiness. [7,1]

Use-value in the objective sense is the relation between a thing and the effect it has the capacity to bring about. It is to objective use-value that people refer in employing such terms as the "heating value" or "heating power" of coal. Subjective use-value is not always based on true objective use-value. There are things to which subjective use-value is attached because people erroneously believe that they have the power to bring about a desired effect. On the other hand there are things able to produce a desired effect to which no use-value is attached because people are ignorant of this fact. [7,1]

To prefer and to set aside and the choices and decisions in which they result are not acts of measurement. Action does not measure utility or value; it chooses between alternatives. There is no abstract problem of total utility or total value. There is no ratiocinative operation which could lead from the valuation of a definite quantity or number of things to the determination of the value of a greater or smaller quantity or number. There is no means of calculating the total value of a supply if only the values of its parts are known. There is no means of establishing the value of a part of a supply if only the value of the total supply is known. There are in the sphere of values and valuations no arithmetical operations; there is no such thing as a calculation of values. [7,1]The law of marginal utility does not refer to objective use-value, but to subjective use-value. It does not deal with the physical or chemical capacity of things to bring about a definite effect in general, but with their relevance for the well-being of a man as he himself sees it under the prevailing momentary state of his affairs. It does not deal primarily with the value of things, but with the value of the services a man expects to get from them. [7,1]

Exchange and profit

Action is an attempt to substitute a more satisfactory state of affairs for a less satisfactory one. We call such a willfully induced alteration an exchange. A less desirable condition is bartered for a more desirable. What gratifies less is abandoned in order to attain something that pleases more. That which is abandoned is called the price paid for the attainment of the end sought. The value of the price paid is called costs. Costs are equal to the value attached to the satisfaction which one must forego in order to attain the end aimed at. [4,4]

The difference between the value of the price paid (the costs incurred) and that of the goal attained is called gain or profit or net yield. Profit in this primary sense is purely subjective, it is an increase in the acting man's happiness, it is a psychical phenomenon that can be neither measured nor weighed. There is a more and a less in the removal of uneasiness felt; but how much one satisfaction surpasses another one can only be felt; it cannot be established and determined in an objective way. A judgment of value does not measure, it arranges in a scale of degrees, it grades. It is expressive of an order of preference and sequence, but not expressive of measure and weight. Only the ordinal numbers can be applied to it, but not the cardinal numbers. [4,4]

Profit, in a broader sense, is the gain derived from action; it is the increase in satisfaction (decrease in uneasiness) brought about; it is the difference between the higher value attached to the result attained and the lower value attached to the sacrifices made for its attainment; it, in other words, yield minus costs. To make profit is invariably the aim sought by any action. If an action fails to attain the ends sought, yield either does not exceed costs or lags behind costs. In the latter case the outcome means a loss, a decrease in satisfaction. [15,8]

We cannot even think of a state of affairs in which people act without the intention of attaining psychic profit and in which their actions result neither in psychic profit nor in psychic loss. In the imaginary construction of an evenly rotating economy[6] there are neither money profits nor money losses. But every individual derives a psychic profit from his actions, or else he would not act at all. [15,8]

Awkward mistakes are due to the tendency to look only upon things tangible, visible, and measurable, and to neglect everything else. What the consumer buys is not simply food or calories. He does not want to feed like a wolf, he wants to eat like a man. Food satisfies the appetite of many people the better, the more appetizingly and tastefully it is prepared, the finer the table is set, and the more agreeable the environment is in which the food is consumed. Such things are regarded as of no consequence by a consideration exclusively occupied with the chemical aspects of the process of digestion. But the fact that they play an important role in the determination of food prices is perfectly compatible with the assertion that people prefer, ceteris paribus, to buy in the cheapest market. Whenever a buyer, in choosing between two things which chemists and

6 An imaginary construction where no changes in the market data occur, and the same market transactions are repeated again and again. - See 4.10

technologists deem perfectly equal, prefers the more expensive, he has a reason. If he does not err, he pays for services which chemistry and technology cannot comprehend with their specific methods of investigation. If a man prefers an expensive place to a cheaper one because he likes to sip his cocktails in the neighborhood of a duke, we may remark on his ridiculous vanity. But we must not say that the man's conduct does not aim at an improvement of his own state of satisfaction. [14,3]

It happens again and again that an action does not attain the end sought. Sometimes the result, although inferior to the end aimed at, is still an improvement when compared with the previous state of affairs; then there is still a profit, although a smaller one than that expected. But it can happen that the action produces a state of affairs less desirable than the previous state it was intended to alter. Then the difference between the valuation of the result and the costs incurred is called loss. [4,4]

Time

Action is always directed toward the future; it is essentially and necessarily always a planning and acting for a better future. Its aim is always to render future conditions more satisfactory than they would be without the interference of action. The uneasiness that impels a man to act is caused by a dissatisfaction with expected future conditions as they would probably develop if nothing were done to alter them. In any case action can influence only the future, never the present that with every infinitesimal fraction of a second sinks down into the past. Man becomes conscious of time when he plans to convert a less satisfactory present state into a more satisfactory future state. [5,2]

He who acts distinguishes between the time before the action, the time absorbed by the action, and the time after the action has been finished. He cannot be neutral with regard to the lapse of time. [5,1]

Man is subject to the passing of time. He comes into existence, grows, becomes old, and passes away. His time is scarce. He must economize it as he economizes other scarce factors. [5,3]

The economization of time has a peculiar character because of the uniqueness and irreversibility of the temporal order. The importance of these facts manifests itself in every part of the theory of action. [5,3]

The economization of time is independent of the economization of economic goods and services. Even in the land of Cockaigne man would be forced to economize time, provided he were not immortal and not endowed with eternal youth and indestructible health and vigor. Although all his appetites could be satisfied immediately without any expenditure of labor, he would have to arrange his time schedule, as there are states of satisfaction which are incompatible and cannot be consummated at the same time. For this man, too, time would be scarce and subject to the aspect of sooner and later. [5,3]

A man's individual actions succeed one another. They can never be effected at the same instant; they can only follow one another in more or less rapid succession. There are actions which serve several purposes at one blow. It would be misleading to refer to them as a coincidence of various actions. [5,4]

People have often failed to recognize the meaning of the term "scale of value" and have disregarded the obstacles preventing the assumption of synchronism in the various actions of an individual. They have interpreted a man's various acts as the outcome of a scale of value, independent of these acts and preceding them, and of a previously devised plan whose realization they aim at. The scale of value and the plan to which duration and immutability for a certain period of time were attributed, were hypostatized[7] into the cause and motive of the various individual actions. Synchronism which could not be asserted with regard to various acts was then easily discovered in the scale of value and in the plan. But this overlooks the fact that the scale of value is nothing but a constructed tool of thought. The scale of value manifests itself only in real acting; it can be discerned only from the observation of real acting. It is therefore impermissible to contrast it with real acting and to use it as a yardstick for the appraisal of real actions. [5,4]

---

7 to hypostatize: to consider mental constructs as real objects

It is no less impermissible to differentiate between rational and allegedly irrational acting on the basis of a comparison of real acting with earlier drafts and plans for future actions. It may be very interesting that yesterday goals were set for today's acting other than those really aimed at today. But yesterday's plans do not provide us with any more objective and nonarbitrary standard for the appraisal of today's real acting than any other ideas and norms. [5,4]

Constancy and rationality are entirely different notions. If one's valuations have changed, unremitting faithfulness to the once espoused principles of action merely for the sake of constancy would not be rational but simply stubborn. Only in one respect can acting be constant: in preferring the more valuable to the less valuable. If the valuations change, acting must change also. Faithfulness, under changed conditions, to an old plan would be nonsensical. A logical system must be consistent and free of contradictions because it implies the coexistence of all its parts and theorems. In acting, which is necessarily in the temporal order, there cannot be any question of such consistency. Acting must be suited to purpose, and purposefulness requires adjustment to changing conditions. [5,4]

The valuation of time periods

Action always aims at the removal of future uneasiness, be it only the future of the impending instant. Between the setting in of action and the attainment of the end sought there always elapses a fraction of time, viz., the maturing time in which the seed sown by the action grows to maturity. The most obvious example is provided by agriculture. [18,1]

Only in rare cases does a simple, indivisible and nonrepeated act suffice to attain the end aimed at. As a rule what separates the actor from the goal of his endeavors is more than one step only. He must make many steps. And every further step to be added to those previously made raises anew the question whether or not he should continue marching toward the goal once chosen. Most goals are so far away that only determined persistence leads to them. Persevering action, unflinchingly directed to the end sought, is needed in order to succeed. The total expenditure of time required, i.e., working time plus maturing time, may be called the period of production. The period of production is long in some cases and short in other cases. It is sometimes so short that it can be entirely neglected in practice. [18,1]

The increment in want-satisfaction which the attainment of the end brings about is temporally limited. The result produced extends services only over a period of time which we may call the duration of serviceableness. The duration of serviceableness is shorter with some products and longer with other goods which are commonly called durable goods. Hence acting man must always take into account the period of production and the duration of serviceableness of the product. In estimating the disutility of a project considered he is not only concerned with the expenditure of material factors and labor required, but also with the period of production. In estimating the utility of the expected product he is concerned with the duration of its serviceableness. Of course, the more durable a product is, the greater is the amount of services it renders. But if these services are not cumulatively available on the same date, but extended piecemeal over a certain period of time, the time element, as will be shown, plays a particular role in their evaluation. It makes a difference whether n units of service are rendered on the same date or whether they are stretched over a period of n days in such a way that only one unit is available daily. [18,1]

It is important to realize that the period of production as well as the duration of serviceableness are categories of human action and not concepts constructed by philosophers, economists, and historians as mental tools for their interpretation of events. They are essential elements present in every act of reasoning that precedes and directs action. [18,1]

Action is not concerned with the future in general, but always with a definite and limited fraction of the future. This fraction is limited, on the one side, by the instant in which the action must take place. Where its other end lies depends on the actor's decision and choice. There are people who are concerned with only the impending instant. There are other people whose provident care stretches far beyond the prospective length of their own life. We may call the fraction of future time for which the actor in a definite action wants to provide in some way and to some extent, the period of provision. In the same way in which acting man chooses among various kinds of want-satisfaction within the same fraction of future time, he chooses also between want-satisfaction in the nearer and in the remoter future. Every choice implies also a choice of a period of provision. In making up his mind how to employ the various means available for the removal of uneasiness, man also determines implicitly the period of provision. In the market economy the demand of the consumers also determines the length of the period of provision. [18,1]

It is one of the fundamental data of human life and action that the shortest processes of production, i.e., those with the shortest period of production, do not remove felt uneasiness entirely. If all those goods which these shortest processes can provide are produced, unsatisfied wants remain and incentive to further action is still present. As acting man prefers those processes which, other things being equal, produce the products in the shortest time, only such processes are left for further action which consume more time. People embark upon these more time-consuming processes because they value the increment in satisfaction expected more highly than the disadvantage of waiting longer for their fruits. [18,1]

The postponement of an act of consumption means that the individual prefers the satisfaction which later consumption will provide to the satisfaction which immediate consumption could provide. The choice of a longer period of production means that the actor values the product of the process bearing fruit only at a later date more highly than the products which a process consuming less time could provide. In such deliberations and the resulting choices the period of production appears as waiting time. [18,1]Time preference is a categorial requisite of human action. No mode of action can be thought of in which satisfaction within a nearer period of the future is not – other things being equal – preferred to that in a later period. The very act of gratifying a desire implies that gratification at the present instant is preferred to that at a later instant. He who consumes a nonperishable good instead of postponing consumption for an indefinite later moment thereby reveals a higher valuation of present satisfaction as compared with later satisfaction. If he were not to prefer satisfaction in a nearer period of the future to that in a remoter period, he would never consume and so satisfy wants. He would always accumulate, he would never consume and enjoy. He would not consume today, but he would not consume tomorrow either, as the morrow would confront him with the same alternative. [18,2]

The value of time, i.e., time preference or the higher valuation of want-satisfaction in nearer periods of the future as against that in remoter periods, is an essential element in human action. It determines every choice and every action. There is no man for whom the difference between sooner and later does not count. The time element is instrumental in the formation of all prices of all commodities and services. [18,3]

Uncertainty

The uncertainty of the future is already implied in the very notion of action. That man acts and that the future is uncertain are by no means two independent matters. They are only two different modes of establishing one thing. [6,1]

We may assume that the outcome of all events and changes is uniquely determined by eternal unchangeable laws governing becoming and development in the whole universe. We may consider the necessary connection and interdependence of all phenomena, i.e., their causal concatenation, as the fundamental and ultimate fact. We may entirely discard the notion of undetermined chance. But however that may be, or appear to the mind of a perfect intelligence, the fact remains that to acting man the future is hidden. If man knew the future, he would not have to choose and would not act. He would be like an automaton, reacting to stimuli without any will of his own. [6,1]

Natural science does not render the future predictable. It makes it possible to foretell the results to be obtained by definite actions. But it leaves unpredictable two spheres: that of insufficiently known natural phenomena and that of human acts of choice. Our ignorance with regard to these two spheres taints all human actions with uncertainty. Apodictic[8] certainty is only within the orbit of the deductive system of aprioristic[9] theory. The most that can be attained with regard to reality is probability. [6,1]

Understanding is always based on incomplete knowledge. We may believe we know the motives of the acting men, the ends they are aiming at, and the means they plan to apply for the attainment of these ends. We have a definite opinion with regard to the effects to be expected from the operation of these factors. But this knowledge is defective. We cannot exclude beforehand the possibility that we have erred in the appraisal of their influence or have failed to take into consideration some factors whose interference we did not foresee at all, or not in a correct way. [6,4]

In the real world acting man is faced with the fact that there are fellow men acting on their own behalf as he himself acts. The necessity to adjust his actions to other people's actions makes him a speculator for whom success and failure depend on his greater or lesser ability to understand the future. Every action is speculation. There is in the course of human events no stability and consequently no safety. [6,4]

Rationality

Human action is necessarily always rational. The term "rational action" is therefore pleonastic and must be rejected as such. When applied to the ultimate ends of action, the terms rational and irrational are inappropriate and meaningless. The ultimate end of action is always the satisfaction of some desires of the acting man. Since nobody is in a position to substitute his own value judgments for those of the acting individual, it is vain to pass judgment on other people's aims and volitions. No man is qualified to declare what would make another man hap-

8 apodictic: absolutely certain, insofar as the negation of that statement is not thinkable

9 aprioristic: which follows logically from statements considered as ultimate truths (*a priori*)

pier or less discontented. The critic either tells us what he believes he would aim at if he were in the place of his fellow; or, in dictatorial arrogance blithely disposing of his fellow's will and aspirations, declares what condition of this other man would better suit himself, the critic. [1,4]

It is usual to call an action irrational if it aims, at the expense of "material" and tangible advantages, at the attainment of "ideal" or "higher" satisfactions. In this sense people say, for instance – sometimes with approval, sometimes with disapproval – that a man who sacrifices life, health, or wealth to the attainment of "higher" goods – like fidelity to his religious, philosophical, and political convictions or the freedom and flowering of his nation – is motivated by irrational considerations. However, the striving after these higher ends is neither more nor less rational or irrational than that after other human ends. It is a mistake to assume that the desire to procure the bare necessities of life and health is more rational, natural, or justified than the striving after other goods or amenities. [1,4]

It is arbitrary to consider only the satisfaction of the body's physiological needs as "natural" and therefore "rational" and everything else as "artificial" and therefore "irrational." It is the characteristic feature of human nature that man seeks not only food, shelter, and cohabitation like all other animals, but that he aims also at other kinds of satisfaction. Man has specifically human desires and needs which we may call "higher" than those which he has in common with the other mammals. [1,4]

When applied to the means chosen for the attainment of ends, the terms rational and irrational imply a judgment about the expediency and adequacy of the procedure employed. The critic approves or disapproves of the method from the point of view of whether or not it is best suited to attain the end in question. It is a fact that human reason is not infallible and that man very often errs in selecting and applying means. An action unsuited to the end sought falls short of expectation. It is contrary to purpose, but it is rational, i.e., the outcome of a reasonable – although faulty – deliberation and an attempt – although an ineffectual attempt – to attain a definite goal. [1,4]

With regard to the problem involved in the antithesis, rational and irrational, there is no difference between the natural sciences and the social sciences. Science always is and must be rational. It is the endeavor to attain a mental grasp of the phenomena of the universe by a systematic arrangement of the whole body of available knowledge. However, as has been pointed out above, the analysis of objects into their constituent elements must sooner or later necessarily reach a point beyond which it cannot go. The human mind is not even capable of conceiving a kind of knowledge not limited by an ultimate given inaccessible to further analysis and reduction. The scientific method that carries the mind up to this point is entirely rational. The ultimate given may be called an irrational fact. [1,4]

Freedom

The content of human action, i.e., the ends aimed at and the means chosen and applied for the attainment of these ends, is determined by the personal qualities of every acting man. Individual man is the product of a long line of zoological evolution which has shaped his physiological inheritance. He is born the offspring and the heir of his ancestors, and the precipitate and sediment of all that his forefathers experienced are his biological patrimony. When he is born, he does not enter the world in general as such, but a definite environment. The innate and inherited biological qualities and all that life has worked upon him make a man what he is at any instant of his pilgrimage. They are his fate and destiny. His will is not "free" in the metaphysical sense of this term. It is determined by his background and all the influences to which he himself and his ancestors were exposed. [2,6]

Inheritance and environment direct a man's actions. They suggest to him both the ends and the means. He lives not simply as man in abstracto; he lives as a son of his family, his race, his people, and his age; as a citizen of his country; as a member of a definite social group; as a practitioner of a certain vocation; as a follower of definite religious, metaphysical, philosophical, and political ideas; as a partisan in many feuds and controversies. He does not himself create his ideas and standards of value; he borrows them from other people. His ideology is what his environment enjoins upon him. Only very few men have the gift of thinking new and original ideas and of changing the traditional body of creeds and doctrines. [2,6]

Most of a man's daily behavior is simple routine. He performs certain acts without paying special attention to them. He does many things because he was trained in his childhood to do them, because other people behave in the same way, and because it is customary in his environment. He acquires habits, he develops automatic reactions. But he indulges in these habits only because he welcomes their effects. As soon as he discovers that the pursuit of the habitual way may hinder the attainment of ends considered as more desirable, he changes his attitude. [2,6]

Praxeology in general and economics and catallactics in particular do not contend or assume that man is free in any metaphysical sense attached to the term freedom. Man is unconditionally subject to the natural conditions of his environment. In acting he must adjust himself to the inexorable regularity of natural phenomena. It is precisely the scarcity of the nature-given conditions of his welfare that enjoins upon man the necessity to act. [23,2]

Only within the frame of a social system can a meaning be attached to the term freedom. As a praxeological term, freedom refers to the sphere within which an acting individual is in a position to choose between alternative modes of action. A man is free in so far as he is permitted to choose ends and the means to be used for the attainment of those ends. A man's freedom is most rigidly restricted by the laws of nature as well as by the laws of praxeology. He cannot attain ends which are incompatible with one another. If he chooses to indulge in gratifications that produce definite effects upon the functioning of his body or his mind, he must put up with these consequences. It would be inexpedient to say that man is not free because he cannot enjoy the pleasures of indulgence in certain drugs without being affected by their inevitable results, commonly considered as highly undesirable. [15,6]

Man cannot have both the advantages derived from peaceful cooperation under the principle of the division of labor within society and the license of embarking upon conduct that is bound to disintegrate society. He must choose between the observance of certain rules that make life within society possible and the poverty and insecurity of the "dangerous life" in a state of perpetual warfare among independent individuals. This is no less rigid a law determining the outcome of all human action than are the laws of physics. [15,6]

Yet there is a far-reaching difference between the sequels resulting from a disregard of the laws of nature and those resulting from a disregard of the laws of praxeology. Of course, both categories of law take care of themselves without requiring any enforcement on the part of man. But the effects of a choice made by an individual are different. A man who absorbs poison harms himself alone. But a man who chooses to resort to robbery upsets the whole social order. While he alone enjoys the short-term gains derived from his action, the disastrous long-term effects harm all the people. His deed is a crime because it has detrimental effects on his fellow men. If society were not to prevent such conduct, it would soon become general and put an end to social cooperation and all the boons the latter confers upon everybody. [15,6]

Labor

The employment of the physiological functions and manifestations of human life as a means is called labor. The display of the potentialities of human energy and vital processes which the man whose life they manifest does not use for the attainment of external ends different from the mere running of these processes and from the physiological role they play in the biological consummation of his own vital economy, is not labor; it is simply life. Man works in using his forces and abilities as a means for the removal of uneasiness and in substituting purposeful exploitation of his vital energy for the spontaneous and carefree discharge of his faculties and nerve tensions. Labor is a means, not an end in itself. [7,3]

Every individual has only a limited quantity of energy to expend, and every unit of labor can only bring about a limited effect. Otherwise human labor would be available in abundance; it would not be scarce and it would not be considered as a means for the removal of uneasiness and economized as such. [7,3]

For praxeology it is a datum that men are eager to enjoy leisure and therefore look upon their own capacity to bring about effects with feelings different from those with which they look upon the capacity of material factors of production. Man in considering an expenditure of his own labor investigates not only whether there is no more desirable end for the employment of the quantity of labor in question, but no less whether it would not be more desirable to abstain from any further expenditure of labor. We can express this fact also in calling the attainment of leisure an end of purposeful activity, or an economic good of the first order. In employing this somewhat sophisticated terminology, we must view leisure as any other economic good from the aspect of marginal utility. We must conclude that the first unit of leisure satisfies a desire more urgently felt than the second one, the second one a more urgent desire than the third one, and so on. Reversing this proposition, we get the statement that the disutility of labor felt by the worker increases in a greater proportion than the amount of labor expended. [7,3]

The fundamental praxeological insight that men prefer what satisfies them more to what satisfies them less and that they value things on the basis of their utility does not need to be corrected or complemented by an additional statement concerning the disutility of labor. These propositions already imply the statement that labor is preferred to leisure only in so far as the yield of labor is more urgently desired than the enjoyment of leisure. [7,3]

The unique position which the factor labor occupies in our world is due to its nonspecific character. All nature-given primary factors of production – i.e., all those natural things and forces that man can use for improving his state of well-being – have specific powers and virtues. There are ends for whose attainment they are more suitable, ends for which they are less suitable, and ends for which they are altogether unsuitable. But human labor is both suitable and indispensable for the performance of all thinkable processes and modes of production. [7,3]

It is, of course, impermissible to deal with human labor as such in general. It is a fundamental mistake not to see that men and their abilities to work are different. The work a certain individual can perform is more suitable for some ends, less suitable for other ends, and altogether unsuitable for still other ends. [7,3]

Men do not economize labor in general, but the particular kinds of labor available. Wages are not paid for labor expended, but for the achievements of labor, which differ widely in quality and quantity. The production of each particular product requires the employment of workers able to perform the particular kind of labor concerned. [7,3]

In speaking of the nonspecific character of human labor we certainly do not assert that all human labor is of the same quality. What we want to establish is rather that the differences in the kind of labor required for the production of various commodities are greater than the differences in the inborn capacities of men. The innate inequality of various individuals does not break up the zoological uniformity and homogeneity of the species man to such an extent as to divide the supply of labor into disconnected sections. Thus the potential supply of labor available for the performance of each particular kind of work exceeds the actual demand for such labor. The supply of every kind of specialized labor could be increased by the withdrawal of workers from other branches and their training. The quantity of need satisfaction is in none of the branches of production permanently limited by a scarcity of people capable of performing special tasks. Only in the short run can there emerge a dearth of specialists. In the long run it can be removed by training people who display the innate abilities required. [7,3]

Labor is the most scarce of all primary means of production because it is in this restricted sense nonspecific and because every variety of production requires the expenditure of labor. Thus the scarcity of the other primary means of production – i.e., the nonhuman means of production supplied by nature – becomes for acting man a scarcity of those primary material means of production whose utilization requires the smallest expenditure of labor. It is the supply of labor available that determines to what an extent the factor nature in each of its varieties can be exploited for the satisfaction of needs. [7,3]

We may try to imagine the conditions within a world in which all material factors of production are so fully employed that there is no opportunity to employ all men or to employ all men to the extent that they are ready to work. In such a world labor is abundant; an increase in the supply of labor cannot add any increment whatever to the total amount of production. If we assume that all men have the same capacity and application for work and if we disregard the disutility of labor, labor in such a world would not be an economic good. If this world were a socialist commonwealth, an increase in population figures would be deemed an increase in the number of idle consumers. If it were a market society, wage rates paid would not be enough to prevent starvation. Those seeking employment would be ready to go to work for any wages, however low, even if insufficient for the preservation of their lives. They would be happy to delay for awhile death by starvation. [7,3]

There is no need to dwell upon the paradoxes of this hypothesis and to discuss the problems of such a world. Our world is different. Labor is more scarce than material factors of production. We are not dealing at this point with the problem of optimum population. We are dealing only with the fact that there are material factors of production which remain unused because the labor required is needed for the satisfaction of more urgent needs. In our world there is no abundance, but a shortage of manpower, and there are unused material factors of production, i.e. land, mineral deposits, and even plants and equipment. [7,3]

The division of labor

The fundamental social phenomenon is the division of labor and its counterpart human cooperation. [8,3]

Experience teaches man that cooperative action is more efficient and productive than isolated action of self-sufficient individuals. The natural conditions determining man's life and effort are such that the division of labor increases output per unit of labor expended. These natural facts are: [8,3]

First: the innate inequality of men with regard to their ability to perform various kinds of labor. Second: the unequal distribution of the nature-given, nonhuman opportunities of production on the surface of the earth. One may as well consider these two facts as one and the same fact, namely, the manifoldness of nature which makes the universe a complex of infinite varieties. If the earth's surface were such that the physical conditions of production were the same at every point and if one man were as equal to all other men as is a circle to another with the same diameter in Euclidian geometry, men would not have embarked upon the division of labor. [8,3]

There is still a third fact, viz., that there are undertakings whose accomplishment exceeds the forces of a single man and requires the joint effort of several. Some of them require an expenditure of labor which no single man can perform because his capacity to work is not great enough. Others again could be accomplished by individuals; but the time which they would have to devote to the work would be so long that the result would only be attained late and would not compensate for the labor expended. In both cases only joint effort makes it possible to attain the end sought. [8,3]

The division of labor is the outcome of man's conscious reaction to the multiplicity of natural conditions. On the other hand it is itself a factor bringing about differentiation. It assigns to the various geographic areas specific functions in the complex of the processes of production. It makes some areas urban, others rural; it locates the various branches of manufacturing, mining, and agriculture in different places. Still more important, however, is the fact that it intensifies the innate inequality of men. Exercise and practice of specific tasks adjust individuals better to the requirements of their performance; men develop some of their inborn faculties and stunt the development of others. Vocational types emerge, people become specialists. [8,5]

The division of labor splits the various processes of production into minute tasks, many of which can be performed by mechanical devices. It is this fact that made the use of machinery possible and brought about the amazing improvements in technical methods of production. Mechanization is the fruit of the division of labor, its most beneficial achievement, not its motive and fountain spring. Power-driven specialized machinery could be employed only in a social environment under the division of labor. Every step forward on the road toward the use of more specialized, more refined, and more productive machines requires a further specialization of tasks. [8,5]

Money and economic calculation

Indirect exchange and money

Interpersonal exchange is called indirect exchange if, between the commodities and services the reciprocal exchange of which is the ultimate end of exchanging, one or several media of exchange are interposed. The subject matter of the theory of indirect exchange is the study of the ratio of exchange between the media of exchange on the one hand and the goods and services of all orders on the other hand. The statements of the theory of indirect exchange refer to all instances of indirect exchange and to all things which are employed as media of exchange. [17,1]

A medium of exchange is a good which people acquire neither for their own consumption nor for employment in their own production activities, but with the intention of exchanging it at a later date against those goods which they want to use either for consumption or for production. [17,3]

Money is a medium of exchange. It is the most marketable good which people acquire because they want to offer it in later acts of interpersonal exchange. Money is the thing which serves as the generally accepted and commonly used medium of exchange. This is its only function. All the other functions which people ascribe to money are merely particular aspects of its primary and sole function, that of a medium of exchange. [17,3]

Every piece of money is owned by one of the members of the market economy. The transfer of money from the control of one actor into that of another is temporally immediate and continuous. There is no fraction of time in between in which the money is not a part of an individual's or a firm's cash holding, but just in "circulation." It is unsound to distinguish between circulating and idle money. It is no less faulty to distinguish between circulating money and hoarded money. What is called hoarding is a height of cash holding which – according to the personal opinion of an observer – exceeds what is deemed normal and adequate. However, hoarding is cash holding. Hoarded money is still money and it serves in the hoards the same purposes which it serves in cash holdings called normal. He who hoards money believes that some special conditions make it expedient to accumulate a cash holding which exceeds the amount he himself would keep under different conditions, or other people keep, or an economist censuring his action considers appropriate. That he acts in this way influences the configuration of the demand for money in the same way in which every "normal" demand influences it. [17,3]

On a market there are only individuals or groups of individuals acting in concert. What motivate these actors are their own concerns, not those of the whole market economy. If there is any sense in such notions as volume of trade and velocity of circulation, then they refer to the resultant of the individuals' actions. It is not permissible to resort to these notions in order to explain the actions of the individuals. The first question that catallactics must raise with regard to changes in the total quantity of money available in the market system is how such changes affect the various individuals' conduct. Modern economics does not ask what "iron" or "bread" is worth, but what a definite piece of iron or of bread is worth to an acting individual at a definite date and a definite place. It cannot help proceeding in the same way with regard to money. [17,2]

The demand for money

Media of exchange are economic goods. They are scarce; there is a demand for them. There are on the market people who desire to acquire them and are ready to exchange goods and services against them. Media of exchange have value in exchange. People make sacrifices for their acquisition; they pay "prices" for them. The peculiarity of these prices lies merely in the fact that they cannot be expressed in terms of money. In reference to the vendible goods and services we speak of prices or of money prices. In reference to money we speak of its purchasing power with regard to various vendible goods. [17,3]

There exists a demand for media of exchange because people want to keep a store of them. Every member of a market society wants to have a definite amount of money in his pocket or box, a cash holding or cash balance of a definite height. Sometimes he wants to keep a larger cash holding, sometimes a smaller; in exceptional cases he may even renounce any cash holding. At any rate, the immense majority of people aim not only to own various vendible goods; they want no less to hold money. Their cash holding is not merely a residuum, an unspent margin of their wealth. It is not an unintentional remainder left over after all intentional acts of buying and selling have been consummated. Its amount is determined by a deliberate demand for cash. And as with all other goods, it is the changes in the relation between demand for and supply of money that bring about changes in the exchange ratio between money and the vendible goods. [17,3]

Money is neither an abstract numeraire nor a standard of value or prices. It is necessarily an economic good and as such it is valued and appraised on its own merits, i.e., the services which a man expects from holding cash. On the market there is always change and movement. Only because there are fluctuations is there money. Money is an element of change not because it "circulates," but because it is kept in cash holdings. Only because people expect changes about the kind and extent of which they have no certain knowledge whatsoever, do they keep money. [17,5]

Where there is no uncertainty concerning the future, there is no need for any cash holding. As money must necessarily be kept by people in their cash holdings, there cannot be any money. The use of media of exchange and the keeping of cash holdings are conditioned by the changeability of economic data. Money in itself is an element of change; its existence is incompatible with the idea of a regular flow of events in an evenly rotating economy. [17,5]

It is true that with regard to money the task of catallactics is broader than with regard to vendible goods. It is not the task of catallactics, but of psychology and physiology, to explain why people are intent on securing the services which the various vendible commodities can render. It is a task of catallactics, however, to deal with this question with regard to money. Catallactics alone can tell us what advantages a man expects from holding money. But it is not these expected advantages which determine the purchasing power of money. The eagerness to secure these advantages is only one of the factors in bringing about the demand for money. It is demand, a subjective element whose intensity is entirely determined by value judgments, and not any objective fact, any power to bring about a certain effect, that plays a role in the formation of the market's exchange ratios. [17,2]

The purchasing power of money

The purchasing power of money is determined by demand and supply, as is the case with the prices of all vendible goods and services. As action always aims at a more satisfactory arrangement of future conditions, he who considers acquiring or giving away money is, of course, first of all interested in its future purchasing power and the future structure of prices. But he cannot form a judgment about the future purchasing power of money otherwise than by looking at its configuration in the immediate past. It is this fact that radically distinguishes the determination of the purchasing power of money from the determination of the mutual exchange ratio between the various vendible goods and services. [17,4]

Today's money relation, as it is shaped on the ground of yesterday's purchasing power, determines today's purchasing power. He who wants to increase his cash holding restricts his purchases and increases his sales and thus brings about a tendency toward falling prices. He who wants to reduce his cash holding increases his purchases – either for consumption or for production and investment – and restricts his sales; thus he brings about a tendency toward rising prices. [17,4]

If all human conditions were unchangeable, if all people were always to repeat the same actions because their uneasiness and their ideas about its removal were constant, or if we were in a position to assume that changes in these factors occurring with some individuals or groups are always outweighed by opposite changes with other individuals or groups and therefore do not effect total demand and total supply, we would live in a world of stability. But the idea that in such a world money's purchasing power could change is contradictory. As will be shown later, changes in the purchasing power of money must necessarily affect the prices of different commodities and services at different times and to different extents; they must consequently bring about changes in demand and supply, in production and consumption. The idea implied in the inappropriate term "level of prices", as if – other things being equal – all prices could rise or drop evenly, is untenable. Other things cannot remain equal if the purchasing power of money changes. [12,4]

In the field of praxeology and economics no sense can be given to the notion of measurement. In the hypothetical state of rigid conditions there are no changes to be measured. In the actual world of change there are no fixed points, dimensions, or relations which could serve as a standard. The monetary unit's purchasing power never changes evenly with regard to all things vendible and purchasable. The notions of stability and stabilization are empty if they do not refer to a state of rigidity and its preservation. However, this state of rigidity cannot even be thought out consistently to its ultimate logical consequences; still less can it be realized. Where there is action, there is change. Action is a lever of change. [12,4]

While money can be thought of only in a changing economy, it is in itself an element of further changes. Every change in the economic data sets it in motion and makes it the driving force of new changes. Every shift in the mutual relation of the exchange ratios between the various nonmonetary goods not only brings about changes in production and in what is popularly called distribution, but also provokes changes in the money relation and thus further changes. Nothing can happen in the orbit of vendible goods without affecting the orbit of money, and all that happens in the orbit of money affects the orbit of commodities. [17,5]

It is therefore neither strange nor vicious that in the frame of such a changing world money is neither neutral nor stable in purchasing power. All plans to render money neutral and stable are contradictory. Money is an element of action and consequently of change. Changes in the money relation, i.e., in the relation of the demand for and the supply of money, effect the exchange ratio between money on the one hand and the vendible commodities on the other hand. These changes do not affect at the same time and to the same extent the prices of the various commodities and services. They consequently affect the wealth of the various members of society in a different way. [17,5]

The supply of money

An increase in the quantity of goods produced, other things being unchanged, must bring about an improvement in people's conditions. Its consequence is a fall in the money prices of the goods the production of which has been increased. But such a fall in money prices does not in the least impair the benefits derived from the additional wealth produced. One may consider as unfair the increase in the share of the additional wealth which goes to the creditors, although such criticisms are questionable as far as the rise in purchasing power has been correctly anticipated and adequately taken into account by a negative price premium. But one must not say that a fall in prices caused by an increase in the production of the goods concerned is the proof of some disequilibrium which cannot be eliminated otherwise than by increasing the quantity of money. [17,10]

Changes in the supply of money must necessarily alter the disposition of vendible goods as owned by various individuals and firms. The quantity of money available in the whole market system cannot increase or decrease otherwise than by first increasing or decreasing the cash holdings of certain individual members. [17,4]

Let us assume that the government issues an additional quantity of paper money. The government plans either to buy commodities and services or to repay debts incurred or to pay interest on such debts. However this may be, the treasury enters the market with an additional demand for goods and services; it is now in a position to buy more goods than it could buy before. The prices of the commodities it buys rise. If the government had expended in its purchases money collected by taxation, the taxpayers would have restricted their purchases and, while the prices of goods bought by the government would have risen, those of other goods would have dropped. [17,4]

But this fall in the prices of the goods the taxpayers used to buy does not occur if the government increases the quantity of money at its disposal without reducing the quantity of money in the hands of the public. The prices of some commodities – viz., of those the government buys – rise immediately, while those of the other commodities remain unaltered for the time being. But the process goes on. Those selling the commodities asked for by the government are now themselves in a position to buy more than they used previously. The prices of the things these people are buying in larger quantities therefore rise too. Thus the boom spreads from one group of commodities and services to other groups until all prices and wage rates have risen. The rise in prices is thus not synchronous for the various commodities and services. [17,4]

When eventually, in the further course of the increase in the quantity of money, all prices have risen, the rise does not affect the various commodities and services to the same extent. For the process has affected the material position of various individuals to different degrees. While the process is under way, some people enjoy the benefit of higher prices for the goods or services they sell, while the prices of the things they buy have not yet risen or have not risen to the same extent. On the other hand, there are people who are in the unhappy situation of selling commodities and services whose prices have not yet risen or not in the same degree as the prices of the goods they must buy for their daily consumption. For the former the progressive rise in prices is a boon, for the latter a calamity. Besides, the debtors are favored at the expense of the creditors. [17,4]

When the process once comes to an end, the wealth of various individuals has been affected in different ways and to different degrees. Some are enriched, some impoverished. Conditions are no longer what they were before. The new order of things results in changes in the intensity of demand for various goods. The mutual ratio of the money prices of the vendible goods and services is no longer the same as before. The price structure has changed apart from the fact that all prices in terms of money have risen. The final prices to the establishment of which the market tends after the effects of the increase in the quantity of money have been fully consummated are not equal to the previous final prices multiplied by the same multiplier. [17,4]

But the purchasing power handed down from the immediate past is modified by today's demand for and supply of money. Human action is always providing for the future, be it sometimes only the future of the impending hour. He who buys, buys for future consumption and production. As far as he believes that the future will differ from the present and the past, he modifies his valuation and appraisement. This is no less true with regard to money than it is with regard to all vendible goods. In this sense we may say that today's exchange value of money is an anticipation of tomorrow's exchange value. The basis of all judgments concerning money is its purchasing power as it was in the immediate past. But as far as cash-induced changes in purchasing power are expected, a second factor enters the scene, the anticipation of these changes. [17,8]

He who believes that the prices of the goods in which he takes an interest will rise, buys more of them than he would have bought in the absence of this belief: accordingly he restricts his cash holding. He who believes that prices will drop, restricts his purchases and thus enlarges his cash holding. As long as such speculative anticipations are limited to some commodities, they do not bring about a general tendency toward changes in cash holding. But it is different if people believe that they are on the eve of big cash-induced changes in purchasing power. When they expect that the money prices of all goods will rise or fall, they expand or restrict their purchases. These attitudes strengthen and accelerate the expected tendencies considerably. This goes on until the point is reached beyond which no further changes in the purchasing power of money are expected. Only then does this inclination to buy or to sell stop and do people begin again to increase or to decrease their cash holdings. [17,8]

But if once public opinion is convinced that the increase in the quantity of money will continue and never come to an end, and that consequently the prices of all commodities and services will not cease to rise, everybody becomes eager to buy as much as possible and to restrict his cash holding to a minimum size. For under these circumstances the regular costs incurred by holding cash are increased by the losses caused by the progressive fall in purchasing power. The advantages of holding cash must be paid for by sacrifices which are deemed unreasonably burdensome. [17,8]

The characteristic mark of this phenomenon is that the increase in the quantity of money causes a fall in the demand for money. The tendency toward a fall in purchasing power as generated by the increased supply of money is intensified by the general propensity to restrict cash holdings which it brings about. Eventually a point is reached where the prices at which people would be prepared to part with "real" goods discount to such an extent the expected progress in the fall of purchasing power that nobody has a sufficient amount of cash at hand to pay them. The monetary system breaks down; all transactions in the money concerned cease; a panic makes its purchasing power vanish altogether. People return either to barter or to the use of another kind of money. [17,8]

The money-substitutes

Claims to a definite amount of money, payable and redeemable on demand, against a debtor about whose solvency and willingness to pay there does not prevail the slightest doubt, render to the individual all the services money can render, provided that all parties with whom he could possibly transact business are perfectly familiar with these essential qualities of the claims concerned: daily maturity as well as undoubted solvency and willingness to pay on the part of the debtor. We may call such claims money-substitutes, as they can fully replace money in an individual's or a firm's cash holding. The technical and legal features of the money-substitutes do not concern catallactics. A money-substitute can be embodied either in a banknote or in a demand deposit with a bank subject to check ("checkbook money" or deposit currency), provided the bank is prepared to exchange the note or the deposit daily free of charge against money proper. Token coins are also money-substitutes, provided the owner is in a position to exchange them at need, free of expense and without delay, against money. [17,11]

People deal with money-substitutes as if they were money because they are fully confident that it will be possible to exchange them at any time without delay and without cost against money. We may call those who share in this confidence and are therefore ready to deal with money-substitutes as if they were money, the clients of the issuing banker, bank, or authority. [17,12]

If the debtor – the government or a bank – keeps against the whole amount of money-substitutes a 100% reserve of money proper, we call the money-substitute a money-certificate. The individual money-certificate is – not necessarily in a legal sense, but always in the catallactic sense – a representative of a corresponding amount of money dept in the reserve. The issuing of money-certificates does not increase the quantity of things suitable to satisfy the demand for money for cash holding. Changes in the quantity of money-certificates therefore do not alter the supply of money and the money relation. They do not play any role in the determination of the purchasing power of money. [17,11]

If the money reserve kept by the debtor against the money-substitutes issued is less than the total amount of such substitutes, we call that amount of substitutes which exceeds the reserve fiduciary media. As a rule it is not possible to ascertain whether a concrete specimen of money-substitutes is a money-certificate or a fiduciary medium. A part of the total amount of money-substitutes issued is usually covered by a money reserve held. Thus a part of the total amount of money-substitutes issued is money certificates, the rest fiduciary media. But this fact can only be recognized by those familiar with the bank's balance sheets. The individual banknote, deposit, or token coin does not indicate its catallactic character. [17,11]

The issue of money-certificates does not increase the funds which the bank can employ in the conduct to its lending business. A bank which does not issue fiduciary media can only grant commodity credit, i.e., it can only lend its own funds and the amount of money which its customers have entrusted to it. The issue of fiduciary media enlarges the bank's funds available for lending beyond these limits It can now not only grant commodity credit, but also circulation credit, i.e., credit granted out of the issue of fiduciary media. [17,11]

While the quantity of money-certificates is indifferent, the quantity of fiduciary media is not. The fiduciary media affect the market phenomena in the same way as money does. Changes in their quantity influence the determination of money's purchasing power and of prices and – temporarily – also of the rate of interest. [17,11]

A bank can never issue more money-substitutes than its clients can keep in their cash holdings. The individual client can never keep a larger portion of his total cash holding in money-substitutes than that corresponding to the proportion which his turnover with other clients of his bank bears to his total turnover. For considerations of convenience he will, as a rule, remain far below this maximum proportion. Thus a limit is drawn to the issue of fiduciary media. We may admit that everybody is ready to accept in his current transactions indiscriminately banknotes issued by any bank and checks drawn upon any bank. But he deposits without delay with his own bank not only the checks but also the banknotes of banks of which he is not himself a client. In the further course his bank settles its accounts with the bank engaged. [17,12]

The term credit expansion has often been misinterpreted. It is important to realize that commodity credit cannot be expanded. The only vehicle of credit expansion is circulation credit. But the granting of circulation credit does not always mean credit expansion. If the amount of fiduciary media previously issued has consummated all its effects upon the market, if prices, wage rates, and interest rates have been adjusted to the total supply of money proper plus fiduciary media (supply of money in the broader sense), granting of circulation credit without a further increase in the quantity of fiduciary media is no longer credit expansion. Credit expansion is present only if credit is granted by the issue of an additional amount of fiduciary media, not if banks lend anew fiduciary media paid back to them by the old debtors. [17,11]

Economic calculation

Acting man uses knowledge provided by the natural sciences for the elaboration of technology, the applied science of action possible in the field of external events. Technology shows what could be achieved if one wanted to achieve it, and how it could be achieved provided people were prepared to employ the means indicated. [11,3]

The means can only be substituted for one another within narrow limits; they are more or less specific means for the attainment of various ends. But, on the other hand, most means are not absolutely specific; most of them are fit for various purposes. The facts that there are different classes of means, that most of the means are better suited for the realization of some ends, less suited for the attainment of some other ends and absolutely useless for the production of a third group of ends, and that therefore the various means allow for various uses, set man the task of allocating them to those employments in which they can render the best service. [11,3]

The art of engineering can establish how a bridge must be built in order to span a river at a given point and to carry definite loads. But it cannot answer the question whether or not the construction of such a bridge would withdraw material factors of production and labor from an employment in which they could satisfy needs more urgently felt. It cannot tell whether or not the bridge should be built at all, where it should be built, what capacity for bearing burdens it should have, and which of the many possibilities for its construction should be chosen. Technological computation can establish relations between various classes of means only to the extent that they can be substituted for one another in the attempts to attain a definite goal. But action is bound to discover relations among all means, however dissimilar they may be, without any regard to the question whether or not they can replace one another in performing the same services. [11,3]

Technology and the considerations derived from it would be of little use for acting man if it were impossible to introduce into their schemes the money prices of goods and services. The projects and designs of engineers would be purely academic if they could not compare input and output on a common basis. The lofty theorist in the seclusion of his laboratory does not bother about such trifling things; what he is searching for is causal relations between various elements of the universe. But the practical man, eager to improve human conditions by removing uneasiness as far as possible, must know whether, under given conditions, what he is planning is the best method, or even a method, to make people less uneasy. He must know whether what he wants to achieve will be an improvement when compared with the present state of affairs and with the advantages to be expected from the execution of other technically realizable projects which cannot be put into execution if the project he has in mind absorbs the available means. Such comparisons can only be made by the use of money prices. [11,3]

Thus money becomes the vehicle of economic calculation. This is not a separate function of money. Money is the universally used medium of exchange, nothing else. Only because money is the common medium of exchange, because most goods and services can be sold and bought on the market against money, and only as far as this is the case, can men use money prices in reckoning. The exchange ratios between money and the various goods and services as established on the market of the past and as expected to be established on the market of the future are the mental tools of economic planning. Where there are no money prices, there are no such things as economic quantities. There are only various quantitative relations between various causes and effects in the external world. There is no means for man to find out what kind of action would best serve his endeavors to remove uneasiness as far as possible. [11,3]

Monetary calculation is the guiding star of action under the social system of division of labor. It is the compass of the man embarking upon production. He calculates in order to distinguish the remunerative lines of production from the unprofitable ones, those of which the sovereign consumers are likely to approve form those of which they are likely to disapprove. Every single step of entrepreneurial activities is subject to scrutiny by monetary calculation. The premeditation of planned action becomes commercial precalculation of expected costs and expected proceeds. The retrospective establishment of the outcome of past action becomes accounting of profit and loss. [13,1]

The prices of the market are the ultimate fact for economic calculation. It cannot be applied for considerations whose standard is not the demand of the consumers as manifested on the market but the hypothetical valuations of a dictatorial body managing all national or earthly affairs. He who seeks to judge actions from the point of view of a pretended "social value," i.e., from the point of view of the "whole society," and to criticize them by comparison with the events in an imaginary socialist system in which his own will is supreme, has no use for economic calculation. Economic calculation in terms of money prices is the calculation of entrepreneurs producing for the consumers of a market society. It is of no avail for other tasks. [12,2]

It is possible to determine in terms of money prices the sum of the income or the wealth of a number of people. But it is nonsensical to reckon national income or national wealth. As soon as we embark upon considerations foreign to the reasoning of a man operating within the pale of a market society, we are no longer helped by monetary calculation methods. The attempts to determine in money the wealth of a nation or of the whole of mankind are as childish as the mystic efforts to solve the riddles of the universe by worrying about the dimensions of the pyramid of Cheops. If a business calculation values a supply of potatoes at $100, the idea is that it will be possible to sell it or to replace it against this sum. If a whole entrepreneurial unit is estimated $1,000,000, it means that one expects to sell it for this amount. But what is the meaning of the items in a statement of a nation's total wealth? What is the meaning of the computation's final result? What must be entered into it and what is to be left outside? Is it correct or not to enclose the "value" of the country's climate and the people's innate abilities and acquired skill? The businessman can convert his property into money, but a nation cannot. [12,2]

The market as a condition for economic calculation

The system of economic calculation in monetary terms is conditioned by certain social institutions. It can operate only in an institutional setting of the division of labor and private ownership of the means of production in which goods and services of all orders are bought and sold against a generally used medium of exchange, i.e., money. [13,1]

Monetary calculation is the method of calculating employed by people acting within the frame of society based on private control of the means of production. It is a device of acting individuals; it is a mode of computation designed for ascertaining private wealth and income and private profits and losses of individuals acting on their own behalf within a free enterprise society. All its results refer to the actions of individuals only. When statisticians summarize these results, the outcome shows the sum of the autonomous actions of a plurality of self-directing individuals, but not the effect of the action of a collective body, of a whole, or of a totality. Monetary calculation is entirely inapplicable and useless for any consideration which does not look at things from the point of view of individuals. It involves calculating the individuals' profits, not imaginary "social" values and "social" welfare. [13,1]

The task which acting man wants to achieve by economic calculation is to establish the outcome of acting by contrasting input and output. Economic calculation is either an estimate of the expected outcome of future action or the establishment of the outcome of past action. But the latter does not serve merely historical and didactic aims. Its practical meaning is to show how much one is free to consume without impairing the future capacity to produce. It is with regard to this problem that the fundamental notions of economic calculation – capital and income, profit and loss, spending and saving, cost and yield – are developed. The practical employment of these notions and of all notions derived from them is inseparably linked with the operation of a market in which goods and services of all orders are exchanged against a universally used medium of exchange, viz., money. They would be merely academic, without any relevance for acting within a world with a different structure of action. [11,4]

There are things which are not for sale and for whose acquisition sacrifices other than money and money's worth must be expended. He who wants to train himself for great achievements must employ many means, some of which may require expenditure of money. But the essential things to be devoted to such an endeavor are not purchasable. Honor, virtue, glory, and likewise vigor, health, and life itself play a role in action both as means and as ends, but they do not enter into economic calculation. [12,2]

There are things which cannot at all be evaluated in money, and there are other things which can be appraised in money only with regard to a fraction of the value assigned to them. The appraisal of an old building must disregard its artistic and historical eminence as far as these qualities are not a source of proceeds in money or goods vendible. What touches a man's heart only and does not induce other people to make sacrifices for its attainment remains outside the pale of economic calculation. [12,2]

However, all this does not in the least impair the usefulness of economic calculation. Those things which do not enter into the items of accountancy and calculation are either ends or goods of the first order. No calculation is required to acknowledge them fully and to make due allowance for them. All that acting man needs in order to make his choice is to contrast them with the total amount of costs their acquisition or preservation requires. [12,2]

There are people to whom monetary calculation is repulsive. They do not want to be roused from their daydreams by the voice of critical reason. Reality sickens them, they long for a realm of unlimited opportunity. They are disgusted by the meanness of a social order in which everything is nicely reckoned in dollars and pennies. They call their grumbling the noble deportment worthy of the friends of the spirit, of beauty, and virtue as opposed to the ignoble baseness and villainy of Babbittry. However, the cult of beauty and virtue, wisdom and the search for truth are not hindered by the rationality of the calculating and computing mind. It is only romantic reverie that cannot thrive in a milieu of sober criticism. The cool-headed reckoner is the stern chastiser of the ecstatic visionary. [13,1]

The fact that the masses prefer detective stories to poetry and that it therefore pays better to write the former than the latter, is not caused by the use of money and monetary accounting. It is not the fault of money that there are gangsters, thieves, murderers, prostitutes, corruptible officials and judges. It is not true that honesty does not "pay." It pays for those who prefer fidelity to what they consider to be right to the advantages which they could derive from a different attitude. [12,2]

Our civilization is inseparably linked with our methods of economic calculation. It would perish if we were to abandon this most precious intellectual tool of acting. [13,1]

Capital and interest

Capital goods

There is an impulse inwrought in all living beings that directs them toward the assimilation of matter that preserves, renews, and strengthens their vital energy. The eminence of acting man is manifested in the fact that he consciously and purposefully aims at maintaining and enhancing his vitality. In the pursuit of this aim his ingenuity leads him to the construction of tools that first aid him in the appropriation of food, then, at a later stage, induce him to design methods of increasing the quantity of foodstuffs available, and finally, enable him to provide for the satisfaction of the most urgently felt among those desires that are specifically human. [15,2]

At the outset of every step forward on the road to a more plentiful existence is saving – the provisionment of products that makes it possible to prolong the average period of time elapsing between the beginning of the production process and its turning out of a product ready for use and consumption. The products accumulated for this purpose are either intermediary stages in the technological process, i.e. tools and half-finished products, or goods ready for consumption that make it possible for man to substitute, without suffering want during the waiting period, a more time-absorbing process for another absorbing a shorter time. These goods are called capital goods. Thus, saving and the resulting accumulation of capital goods are at the beginning of every attempt to improve the material conditions of man; they are the foundation of human civilization. Without saving and capital accumulation there could not be any striving toward non-material ends. [15,2]

Capital goods are intermediary products which in the further course of production activities are transformed into consumers' goods. All capital goods, including those not called perishable, perish either in wearing out their serviceableness in the performance of production processes or in losing their serviceableness, even before this happens, through a change in the market data. There is no question of keeping a stock of capital goods intact. They are transient. [18,7]

It is necessary to realize that all economic categories are related to human action and have nothing at all to do directly with the physical properties of things. Economics is not about goods and services; it is about human choice and action. The praxeological concept of time is not the concept of physics or biology. It refers to the sooner or the later as operative in the actors' judgments of value. The distinction between capital goods and consumers' goods is not a rigid distinction based on the physical and physiological properties of the goods concerned. It depends on the position of the actors and the choices they have to make. The same goods can be looked upon as capital goods or as consumers' goods. A supply of goods ready for immediate enjoyment is capital goods from the point of view of a man who looks upon it as a means for his own sustenance and that of hired workers during a waiting time. [18,4]

Capital

From the notion of capital goods one must clearly distinguish the concept of capital. The concept of capital is the fundamental concept of economic calculation, the foremost mental tool of the conduct of affairs in the market economy. Its correlative is the concept of income. [15,2]

There is no such thing as an abstract or ideal capital that exists apart from concrete capital goods. If we disregard the role cash holding plays in the composition of capital, we must realize that capital is always embodied in definite capital goods and is affected by everything that happens with regard to them.

The value of an amount of capital is a derivative of the value of the capital goods in which it is embodied. The money equivalent of an amount of capital is the sum of the money equivalents of the aggregate of capital goods to which one refers in speaking of capital in the abstract. There is nothing which could be called "free" capital. Capital is always in the form of definite capital goods. [18,5]

The idea of capital has no counterpart in the physical universe of tangible things. It is nowhere but in the minds of planning men. It is an element in economic calculation. Capital accounting serves one purpose only. It is designed to make us know how our arrangement of production and consumption acts upon our power to satisfy future wants. The question it answers is whether a certain course of conduct increases or decreases the productivity of our future exertion. [18,7]

Capital is a praxeological concept. It is a product of reasoning, and its place is in the human mind. It is a mode of looking at the problems of acting, a method of appraising them from the point of view of a definite plan. It determines the course of human action and is, in this sense only, a real factor. It is inescapably linked with capitalism, the market economy. [18,7]

Capital accounting

Capital accounting starts with the market prices of the capital goods available for further production, the sum of which it calls capital. It records every expenditure from this fund and the price of all incoming items induced by such expenditures. It establishes finally the ultimate outcome of all these transformations in the composition of the capital and thereby the success or the failure of the whole process. It shows not only the final result; it mirrors also every one of its intermediary stages. It produces interim balances for every day such a balance may be required and statements of profit and loss for every part or stage of the process. It is the indispensable compass of production in the market economy. [18,3]

Capital accounting is a mental tool of calculating and computing suitable for individuals and groups of individuals acting in the market economy. Only in the frame of monetary calculation can capital become computable. The sole task that capital accounting can perform is to show to the various individuals acting within a market economy whether the money equivalent of their funds devoted to acquisitive action has changed and to what extent. For all other purposes capital accounting is quite useless. [18,9]

In the market economy production is a continuous, never-ending pursuit split up into an immense variety of partial processes. Innumerable processes of production with different periods of production are in progress simultaneously. They complement one another and at the same time are in rivalry with one another in competing for scarce factors of production. Continuously either new capital is accumulated by saving or previously accumulated capital is eaten up by overconsumption. Production is distributed among numerous individual plants, farms, workshops, and enterprises each of which serves only limited purposes. The intermediary products or capital goods, the produced factors of further production, change hands in the course of events; they pass from one plant to another until finally the consumers' goods reach those who use and enjoy them. The social process of production never stops. At each instant numberless processes are in progress some of which are nearer to, some remoter from, the achievement of their special tasks. [18,3]

The businessman, the acting man, is entirely absorbed in one task only: to take best advantage of all the means available for the improvement of future conditions. He does not look at the present state of affairs with the aim of analyzing and comprehending it. In classifying the means for further production and appraising their importance he adopts superficial rules of thumb. He distinguishes three classes of factors of production: the nature-given material factors, the human factor – labor, and capital goods – the intermediary factors produced in the past. He does not analyze the nature of the capital goods. They are in his eyes means of increasing the productivity of labor. Quite naively he ascribes to them productive power of their own. He does not trace their instrumentality back to nature and labor. He does not ask how they came into existence. They count only as far as they may contribute to the success of his efforts. [18,3]

This mode of reasoning is all right for the businessman. But it was a serious mistake for the economists to agree with the businessman's superficial view. They erred in classifying "capital" as an independent factor of production along with the nature-given material resources and labor. The capital goods – the factors of further production produced in the past – are not an independent factor. They are the joint products of the cooperation of the two original factors – nature and labor – expended in the past. They have no productive power of their own. [18,3]

The sale and purchase of capital goods and the loans granted to business are not as such capital transfer. They are transactions which are instrumental in conveying the concrete capital goods into the hands of those entrepreneurs who want to employ them for the performance of definite projects. They are only ancillary steps in the course of a long-range sequence of acts. Their composite effect decides the success or failure of the whole project. But neither profit nor loss directly brings about either capital accumulation or capital consumption. It is the way in which those in whose fortune profit or loss occurs arrange their consumption that alters the amount of capital available. [18,7]

Capital consumption and the physical extinction of capital goods are two different things. All capital goods sooner or later enter into final products and cease to exist through use, consumption, wear and tear. What can be preserved by an appropriate arrangement of consumption is only the value of a capital fund, never the concrete capital goods. It may sometimes happen that acts of God or manmade destruction result in so great an extinction of capital goods that no possible restriction of consumption can bring about in a short time a replenishment of the capital funds to its previous level. But what brings about such a depletion is always the fact that the net proceeds of current production devoted to the maintenance of capital are not sufficiently large. [18,7]

The convertibility of capital goods

Capital goods are intermediary steps on the way toward a definite goal. If in the course of the period of production the goal is changed, it is not always possible to use the intermediary products already available for the pursuit of the new goal. Some of the capital goods may become absolutely useless, and all expenditure made in their production appears now as waste. Other capital goods could be utilized for the new project but only after having been subjected to a process of adjustment; it would have been possible to spare the costs required by this alteration if one had from the start aimed at the new goal. A third group of capital goods can be employed for the new process without any alteration; but if it had been known at the time they were produced that they would be used in the new way, it would have been possible to manufacture at smaller cost other goods which could render the same service. Finally there are also capital goods which can be employed for the new project just as well as for the original one. [18,5]

The more a definite process of production approaches its ultimate end, the closer becomes the tie between its intermediary products and the goal aimed at. Iron is less specific in character than iron tubes, and iron tubes less so than iron machine-parts. The conversion of a process of production becomes as a rule the more difficult, the farther it has been pursued and the nearer it has come to its termination, the turning out of consumers' goods. [18,5]

Capitalists and entrepreneurs in their capacity as owners of capital are never perfectly free; they are never on the eve of the first decision and action which will bind them. They are always already engaged in some way or other. Their funds are not outside the social process of production, but invested in definite lines. If they own cash, this is, according to the state of the market, either a sound or an unsound "investment"; but it is always an investment. They have either let slip the right moment for the purchase of concrete factors of production which they must buy sooner or later, or the right moment to buy has not yet come. In the first case their holding of cash is unsound;

they have missed an opportunity. In the second case their choice was correct. [18,5]

Capitalists and entrepreneurs in expending money for the purchase of concrete factors of production value the goods exclusively from the point of view of the anticipated future state of the market. They pay prices adjusted to future conditions as they themselves appraise them today. Errors committed in the past in the production of capital goods available today do not burden the buyer; their incidence falls entirely on the seller. In this sense the entrepreneur who proceeds to buy against money capital goods for future production crosses out the past. His entrepreneurial ventures are not affected by changes which in the past occurred in the valuation and the prices of the factors of production he acquires. In this sense alone one may say that the owner of ready cash owns liquid funds and is free. [18,5]

The more the accumulation of capital goods proceeds, the greater becomes the problem of convertibility. The primitive methods of farmers and handicraftsmen of earlier ages could more easily be adjusted to new tasks than modern capitalist methods. But it is precisely modern capitalism that is faced with rapid changes in conditions. Changes in technological knowledge and in the demand of the consumers as they occur daily in our time make obsolete many of the plans directing the course of production and raise the question whether or not one should pursue the path started on. [18,6]

All material wealth is a residuum of past activities and is embodied in concrete capital goods of limited convertibility. The capital goods accumulated direct the actions of the living into lines which they would not have chosen if their discretion had not been restricted by binding action accomplished in the past. The choice of ends and of the means for the attainment of these ends is influenced by the past. Capital goods are a conservative element. They force us to adjust our actions to conditions brought about by our own conduct in earlier days and by the thinking, choosing and acting of bygone generations. [18,6]

The intermediary products available today were manufactured in the past by our ancestors and by ourselves. The plans which guided their production were an outgrowth of the then prevailing ideas concerning ends and technological procedures. If we consider aiming at different ends and choosing different methods of production, we are faced with an alternative. We must either leave unused a great part of the capital goods available and start afresh producing modern equipment, or we must adjust our production processes as far as possible to the specific character of the capital goods available. The choice rests, as it always does in the market economy, with the consumers. [18,6]

The mobility of the investor

The limited convertibility of the capital goods does not immovably bind their owner. The investor is free to alter the investment of his funds. If he is able to anticipate the future state of the market more correctly than other people, he can succeed in choosing only investments whose price will rise and in avoiding investments whose price will drop. [18,8]

Entrepreneurial profit and loss emanate from the dedication of factors of production to definite projects. Stock exchange speculation and analogous transactions outside the securities market determine on whom the incidence of these profits and losses shall fall. A tendency prevails to make a sharp distinction between such purely speculative ventures and genuinely sound investment. The distinction is one of degree only. There is no such thing as a nonspeculative investment. In a changing economy action always involves speculation. Investments may be good or bad, but they are always speculative. A radical change in conditions may render bad even investments commonly considered perfectly safe. [18,8]

Stock speculation cannot undo past action and cannot change anything with regard to the limited convertibility of capital goods already in existence. What it can do is to prevent additional investment in branches and enterprises in which, according to the opinion of the speculators, it would be misplaced. It points the specific way for a tendency, prevailing in the market economy, to expand profitable production ventures and to restrict the unprofitable. In this sense the stock exchange becomes simply "the market," the focal point of the market economy, the ultimate device to make the anticipated demand of the consumers supreme in the conduct of business. [18,8]

The mobility of the investor manifests itself in the phenomenon misleadingly called capital flight. Individual investors can go away from investments which they consider unsafe provided that they are ready to take the loss already discounted by the market. Thus they can protect themselves against anticipated further losses and shift them to people who are less realistic in their appraisal of the future prices of the goods concerned. Capital flight does not withdraw inconvertible capital goods from the lines of their investment. It consists merely in a change of ownership. [18,8]

It makes no difference in this regard whether the capitalist "flees" into another domestic investment or into a foreign investment. One of the main objectives of foreign exchange control is to prevent capital flight into foreign countries. However, foreign exchange control only succeeds in preventing the owners of domestic investments from restricting their losses by exchanging in time a domestic investment they consider unsafe for a foreign investment they consider safe. [18,8]

Capital flight into a foreign country presupposes the propensity of foreigners to exchange their investments abroad against those in the country from which capital flees. A British capitalist cannot flee from his British investments if no foreigner buys them. It follows that capital flight can never result in the much talked about deterioration of the balance of payments. Neither can it make foreign exchange rates rise. If many capitalists – whether British or foreign – want to get rid of British securities, a drop in their prices will ensue. But it will not affect the exchange ratio between the sterling and foreign currencies. [18,8]

Originary interest

It has been shown that time preference is a category inherent in every human action. Time preference manifests itself in the phenomenon of originary interest, i.e., the discount of future goods as against present goods. [19,1]

Originary interest is the ratio of the value assigned to want-satisfaction in the immediate future and the value assigned to want-satisfaction in remote periods of the future. It manifests itself in the market economy in the discount of future goods as against present goods. It is a ratio of commodity prices, not a price in itself. There prevails a tendency toward the equalization of this ratio for all commodities. In the imaginary construction of the evenly rotating economy the rate of originary interest is the same for all commodities. [19,2]

Originary interest is not a price determined on the market by the interplay of the demand for and the supply of capital or capital goods. Its height does not depend on the extent of this demand and supply. It is rather the rate of originary interest that determines both the demand for and the supply of capital and capital goods. It determines how much of the available supply of goods is to be devoted to consumption in the immediate future and how much to provision for remoter periods of the future. [19,2]

People do not save and accumulate capital because there is interest. Interest is neither the impetus to saving nor the reward or the compensation granted for abstaining from immediate consumption. It is the ratio in the mutual valuation of present goods as against future goods. [19,2]

We cannot even think of a world in which originary interest would not exist as an inexorable element in every kind of action. Whether there is or is not division of labor and social cooperation and whether there is or is not division of labor and social cooperation and whether society is organized on the basis of private or of public control of the means of production, originary interest is always present. [19,2]

As long as the world is not transformed into a land of Cockaigne, men are faced with scarcity and must act and economize; they are forced to choose between satisfaction in nearer and in remoter periods of the future because neither for the former nor for the latter can full contentment be attained. Then a change in the employment of factors of production which withdraws such factors from their employment for want-satisfaction in the nearer future and devotes them to want-satisfaction in the remoter future must necessarily impair the state of satisfaction in the nearer future and improve it in the remoter future. [19,2]

If the means are scarce, if the praxeological correlation of ends and means still exists, there are by logical necessity unsatisfied wants with regard both to nearer and to remoter periods of the future. There are always goods the procurement of which we must forego because the way that leads to their production is too long and would prevent us from satisfying more urgent needs. The fact that we do not provide more amply for the future is the outcome of a weighing of satisfaction in nearer periods of the future against satisfaction in remoter periods of the future. The ratio which is the outcome of this valuation is originary interest. [19,2]

The activities of the entrepreneurs tend toward the establishment of a uniform rate of originary interest in the whole market economy. If there turns up in one sector of the market a margin between the prices of present goods and those of future goods which deviates from the margin prevailing in other sectors, a trend toward equalization is brought about by the striving of businessmen to enter those sectors in which this margin is higher and to avoid those in which it is lower. The final rate of originary interest is the same in all parts of the market of the evenly rotating economy. [19,5]

The market rates of interest

The market rates of interest on loans are not pure interest rates. Among the components contributing to their determination there are also elements which are not interest. The moneylender is always an entrepreneur. Every grant of credit is a speculative entrepreneurial venture, the success or failure of which is uncertain. The lender is always faced with the possibil-

ity that he may lose a part or the whole of the principal lent.
His appraisal of this danger determines his conduct in bargain-
ing with the prospective debtor about the terms of the contract. [20,2]

There can never be perfect safety either in moneylending
or in other classes of credit transactions and deferred payments. Debtors, guarantors, and warrantors may become in-
solvent; collateral[10] and mortgages may become worthless. The
creditor is always a virtual partner of the debtor or a virtual
owner of the pledged and mortgaged property. He can be affected by changes in the market data concerning them. He has
linked his fate with that of the debtor or with the changes occurring in the price of the collateral. Capital as such does not
bear interest; it must be well employed and invested not only in
order to yield interest, but also lest it disappear entirely. [20,2]

In the world of reality all prices are fluctuating and acting men are forced to take full account of these changes. Entrepreneurs embark upon business ventures and capitalists
change their investments only because they anticipate such
changes and want to profit from them. The market economy is
essentially characterized as a social system in which there prevails an incessant urge toward improvement. The most provident and enterprising individuals are driven to earn profit by re-
adjusting again and again the arrangement of production activities so as to fill in the best possible way the needs of the consumers, both those needs of which the consumers themselves
are already aware and those latent needs of the satisfaction of
which they have not yet thought themselves. These speculative
ventures of the promoters revolutionize afresh each day the
structure of prices and thereby also the height of the gross
market rate of interest. [20,3]

He who expects a rise in certain prices enters the loan
market as a borrower and is ready to allow a higher gross rate
of interest than he would allow if he were to expect a less momentous rise in prices or no rise at all. On the other hand, the
lender, if he himself expects a rise in prices, grants loans only if
the gross rate is higher than it would be under a state of the

10 collateral: an asset offered as a guarantee of a loan

market in which less momentous or no upward changes in prices are anticipated. The borrower is not deterred by a higher rate if his project seems to offer such good chances that it can afford higher costs. The lender would abstain from lending and would himself enter the market as an entrepreneur and bidder for commodities and services if the gross rate of interest were not to compensate him for the profits he could reap this way. The expectation of rising prices thus has the tendency to make the gross rate of interest rise, while the expectation of dropping prices makes it drop. If the expected changes in the price structure concern only a limited group of commodities and services, and are counterbalanced by the expectation of an opposite change in the prices of other goods, as is the case in the absence of changes in the money relation, the two opposite trends by and large counterpoise each other. But if the money relation is sensibly altered and a general rise or fall in prices of all commodities and services is expected, one tendency carries on. A positive or negative price premium emerges in all deals concerning deferred payments. [20,3]

The emergence of the price premium is not the product of an arithmetical operation which could provide reliable knowledge and eliminate the uncertainty concerning the future. It is the outcome of the promoters' understanding of the future and their calculations based on such an understanding. It comes into existence step by step as soon as first a few and then successively more and more actors become aware of the fact that the market is faced with cash-induced changes in the money relation and consequently with a trend orientated in a definite direction. Only when people begin to buy or to sell in order to take advantage of this trend, does the price premium come into existence. [20,3]

It is necessary to realize that the price premium is the outgrowth of speculations anticipating changes in the money relation. What induces it, in the case of the expectation that an inflationary trend will keep on going, is already the first sign of that phenomenon which later, when it becomes general, is called "flight into real values" and finally produces the crack-up boom and the crash of the monetary system concerned. As in every case of the understanding of future developments, it is possible that the speculators may err, that the inflationary or deflationary movement will be stopped or slowed down, and that prices will differ from what they expected. [20,3]

Business cycles

Credit expansion

In analyzing the process of credit expansion, let us assume that the economic system's process of adjustment to the market data and of movement toward the establishment of final prices and interest rates is disturbed by the appearance of a new datum, namely, an additional quantity of fiduciary media offered on the loan market. At the gross market rate which prevailed on the eve of this disturbance, all those who were ready to borrow money at this rate, due allowance being made for the entrepreneurial component in each case, could borrow as much as they wanted. [20,6]

A drop in the gross market rate of interest affects the entrepreneur's calculation concerning the chances of the profitability of projects considered. Along with the prices of the material factors of production, wage rates, and the anticipated future prices of the products, interest rates are items that enter into the planning businessman's calculation. The result of this calculation shows the businessman whether or not a definite project will pay. It shows him what investments can be made under the given state of the ratio in the public's valuation of future goods as against present goods. It brings his actions into agreement with this valuation. It prevents him from embarking upon projects the realization of which would be disapproved by the public because of the length of the waiting time they require. It forces him to employ the available stock of capital goods in such a way as to satisfy best the most urgent wants of the consumers. [20,6]

But now the drop in interest rates falsifies the business-man's calculation. Although the amount of capital goods available did not increase, the calculation employs figures which would be utilizable only if such an increase had taken place. The result of such calculations is therefore misleading. They make some projects appear profitable and realizable which a correct calculation, based on an interest rate not manipulated by credit expansion, would have shown as unrealizable. Entrepreneurs embark upon the execution of such projects. Business activities are stimulated. A boom begins. [20,6]

The boom

The additional demand on the part of the expanding entrepreneurs tends to raise the prices of producers' goods and wage rates. With the rise in wage rates, the prices of consumers' goods rise too. Besides, the entrepreneurs are contributing a share to the rise in the prices of consumers' goods as they too, deluded by the illusory gains which their business accounts show, are ready to consume more. The general upswing in prices spreads optimism. If only the prices of producers' goods had risen and those of consumers' goods had not been affected, the entrepreneurs would have become embarrassed. They would have had doubts concerning the soundness of their plans, as the rise in costs of production would have upset their calculations. But they are reassured by the fact that the demand for consumers' goods is intensified and makes it possible to expand sales in spite of rising prices. Thus they are confident that production will pay, notwithstanding the higher costs it involves. They are resolved to go on. [20,6]

Of course, in order to continue production on the enlarged scale brought about by the expansion of credit, all entrepreneurs, those who did expand their activities no less than those who produce only within the limits in which they produced previously, need additional funds as the costs of production are now higher. If the credit expansion consists merely in a single, not repeated injection of a definite amount of fiduciary media into the loan market and then ceases altogether, the boom must very soon stop. The entrepreneurs cannot procure the funds they need for the further conduct of their ventures. This gross market rate of interest rises because the increased demand for loans is not counterpoised by a corresponding increase in the quantity of money available for lending. Commodity prices drop because some entrepreneurs are selling inventories and others abstain from buying. The size of business activities shrinks again. The boom ends because the forces which brought it about are no longer in operation. [20,6]

The boom can last only as long as the credit expansion progresses at an ever-accelerated pace. The boom comes to an end as soon as additional quantities of fiduciary media are no longer thrown upon the loan market. But it could not last forever even if inflation and credit expansion were to go on endlessly. It would then encounter the barriers which prevent the boundless expansion of circulation credit. It would lead to the crack-up boom and the breakdown of the whole monetary system. [20,6]

It is customary to describe the boom as overinvestment. However, additional investment is only possible to the extent that there is an additional supply of capital goods available. As, apart from forced saving, the boom itself does not result in a restriction but rather in an increase in consumption, it does not procure more capital goods for new investment. The essence of the credit-expansion boom is not overinvestment, but investment in wrong lines, i.e., malinvestment. [20,6]

Technological conditions make it necessary to start an expansion of production by expanding first the size of the plants producing the goods of those orders which are farthest removed from the finished consumers' goods. In order to expand the production of shoes, clothes, motorcars, furniture, houses, one must begin with increasing the production of iron, steel, copper, and other such goods. [20,6]

The whole entrepreneurial class is, as it were, in the position of a master-builder whose task it is to erect a building out of a limited supply of building materials. If this man overestimates the quantity of the available supply, he drafts a plan for the execution of which the means at his disposal are not sufficient. He oversizes the groundwork and the foundations and only discovers later in the progress of the construction that he lacks the material needed for the completion of the structure. It is obvious that our master-builder's fault was not overinvestment, but an inappropriate employment of the means at his disposal. [20,6]

However conditions may be, it is certain that no manipulations of the banks can provide the economic system with capital goods. What is needed for a sound expansion of production is additional capital goods, not money or fiduciary media. The credit expansion boom is built on the sands of banknotes and deposits. It must collapse. [20,6]

The breakdown

The breakdown appears as soon as the banks become frightened by the accelerated pace of the boom and begin to abstain from further expansion of credit. The boom could continue only as long as the banks were ready to grant freely all those credits which business needed for the execution of its excessive projects, utterly disagreeing with the real state of the supply of factors of production and the valuations of the consumers. These illusory plans, suggested by the falsification of business calculation as brought about by the cheap money policy, can be pushed forward only if new credits can be obtained at gross market rates which are artificially lowered below the height they would reach at an unhampered loan market. It is this margin that gives them the deceptive appearance of profitability. The change in the banks' conduct does not create the crisis. It merely makes visible the havoc spread by the faults which business has committed in the boom period. [20,6]

Neither could the boom last endlessly if the banks were to cling stubbornly to their expansionist policies. Any attempt to substitute additional fiduciary media for nonexisting capital goods is doomed to failure. If the credit expansion is not stopped in time, the boom turns into the crack-up boom; the flight into real values begins, and the whole monetary system founders. However, as a rule, the banks in the past have not pushed things to extremes. They have become alarmed at a date when the final catastrophe was still far away. [20,6]

As soon as the afflux of additional fiduciary media comes to an end, the airy castle of the boom collapses. The entrepreneurs must restrict their activities because they lack the funds for their continuation on the exaggerated scale. Prices drop suddenly because these distressed firms try to obtain cash by throwing inventories on the market dirt cheap. Factories are closed, the continuation of construction projects in progress is halted, workers are discharged. As on the one hand many firms badly need money in order to avoid bankruptcy, and on the other hand no firm any longer enjoys confidence, the entrepreneurial component in the gross market rate of interest jumps to an excessive height. [20,6]

Accidental institutional and psychological circumstances generally turn the outbreak of the crisis into a panic. The description of these awful events can be left to the historians. It is not the task of catallactic theory to depict in detail the calamities of panicky days and weeks and to dwell upon their sometimes grotesque aspects. Economics is not interested in what is accidental and conditioned by the individual historical circumstances of each instance. Its aim is, on the contrary, to distinguish what is essential and necessary from what is merely adventitious. It is not interested in the psychological aspects of the panic, but only in the fact that a credit-expansion boom must unavoidably lead to a process which everyday speech calls the depression. It must realize that the depression is in fact the process of readjustment, of putting production activities anew in agreement with the given state of the market data: the available supply of factors of production, the valuations of the consumers, and particularly also the state of originary interest as manifested in the public's valuations. [20,6]

These data, however, are no longer identical with those that prevailed on the eve of the expansionist process. A good many things have changed. Forced saving and, to an even greater extent, regular voluntary saving may have provided new capital goods which were not totally squandered through malinvestment and overconsumption as induced by the boom. Changes in the wealth and income of various individuals and groups of individuals have been brought about by the unevenness inherent in every inflationary movement. Apart from any causal relation to the credit expansion, population may have changed with regard to figures and the characteristics of the individuals comprising them; technological knowledge may have advanced, demand for certain goods may have been altered. The final state to the establishment of which the market tends is no longer the same toward which it tended before the disturbances created by the credit expansion. [20,6]

Some of the investments made in the boom period appear, when appraised with the sober judgment of the readjustment period, no longer dimmed by the illusions of the upswing, as absolutely hopeless failures. They must simply be abandoned because the current means required for their further exploitation cannot be recovered in selling their products; this "circulating" capital is more ungently needed in other branches of want-satisfaction; the proof is that it can be employed in a more profitable way in other fields. Other malinvestments offer somewhat more favorable chances. It is, of course, true that one would not have embarked upon putting capital goods into them if one had correctly calculated. The inconvertible investments made on their behalf are certainly wasted. But as they are inconvertible, a fait accompli, they present further action with a new problem. If the proceeds which the sale of their products promises are expected to exceed the costs of current operation, it is profitable to carry on. Although the prices which the buying public is prepared to allow for their products are not high enough to make the whole of the inconvertible investment profitable, they are sufficient to make a fraction, however small, of the investment profitable. The rest of the investment must be considered as expenditure without any offset, as capital squandered and lost. [20,6]

The consequences

The final outcome of the credit expansion is general impoverishment. Some people may have increased their wealth; they did not let their reasoning be obfuscated by the mass hysteria, and took advantage in time of the opportunities offered by the mobility of the individual investor. Other individuals and groups of individuals may have been favored, without any initiative of their own, by the mere time lag between the rise in the prices of the goods they sell and those they buy. But the immense majority must foot the bill for the malinvestments and the overconsumption of the boom episode. [20,6]

Expansion produces first the illusory appearance of prosperity. It is extremely popular because it seems to make the majority, even everybody, more affluent. It has an enticing quality. A special moral effort is needed to stop it. On the other hand, contraction immediately produces conditions which everybody is ready to condemn as evil. Its unpopularity is even greater than the popularity of expansion. It creates violent opposition. Very soon the political forces fighting it become irresistible. [20,7]

But the dissimilarity between the two opposite modes of money credit manipulation not only consists in the fact that while one of them is popular the other is universally loathed. Deflation and contraction are less likely to spread havoc than inflation and expansion not merely because they are only rarely resorted to. They are less disastrous also on account of their inherent effects. Expansion squanders scarce factors of production by malinvestment and overconsumption. If it once comes to an end, a tedious process of recovery is needed in order to wipe out the impoverishment it has left behind. But contraction produces neither malinvestment nor overconsumption. The temporary restriction in business activities that it engenders may by and large be offset by the drop in consumption on the part of discharged wage earners and the owners of the material factors of production the sales of which drop. No protracted scars are left. When the contraction comes to an end, the process of readjustment does not need to make good for losses caused by capital consumption. [20,7]

The popularity of inflation and credit expansion, the ultimate source of the repeated attempts to render people prosperous by credit expansion, and thus the cause of the cyclical fluctuations of business, manifests itself clearly in the customary terminology. The boom is called good business, prosperity, and upswing. Its unavoidable aftermath, the readjustment of conditions to the real data of the market, is called crisis, slump, bad business, depression. People rebel against the insight that the disturbing element is to be seen in the malinvestment and the overconsumption of the boom period and that such an artificially induced boom is doomed. They are looking for the philosophers' stone to make it last. [20,9]

The boom produces impoverishment. But still more disastrous are its moral ravages. It makes people despondent and dispirited. The more optimistic they were under the illusory prosperity of the boom, the greater is their despair and their feeling of frustration. The individual is always ready to ascribe his good luck to his own efficiency and to take it as a well-deserved reward for his talent, application, and probity. But reverses of fortune he always charges to other people, and most of all to the absurdity of social and political institutions. He does not blame the authorities for having fostered the boom. He reviles them for the inevitable collapse. In the opinion of the public, more inflation and more credit expansion are the only remedy against the evils which inflation and credit expansion have brought about. [20,9]

Out of the collapse of the boom there is only one way back to a state of affairs in which progressive accumulation of capital safeguards a steady improvement of material well-being: new saving must accumulate the capital goods needed for a harmonious equipment of all branches of production with the capital required. One must provide the capital goods lacking in those branches which were unduly neglected in the boom. Wage rates must drop; people must restrict their consumption temporarily until the capital wasted by malinvestment is restored. Those who dislike these hardships of the readjustment period must abstain in time from credit expansion. [20,9]

There is no use in interfering by means of a new credit expansion with the process of readjustment. This would at best only interrupt, disturb, and prolong the curative process of the depression, if not bring about a new boom with all its inevitable consequences. [20,9]

The process of readjustment, even in the absence of any new credit expansion, is delayed by the psychological effects of disappointment and frustration. People are slow to free themselves from the self-deception of delusive prosperity. Businessmen try to continue unprofitable projects; they shut their eyes to an insight that hurts. The workers delay reducing their claims to the level required by the state of the market; they want, if possible, to avoid lowering their standard of living and changing their occupation and their dwelling place. People are the more discouraged the greater their optimism was in the days of the upswing. They have for the moment lost self-confidence and the spirit of enterprise to such an extent that they even fail to take advantage of good opportunities. But the worst is that people are incorrigible. After a few years they embark anew upon credit expansion, and the old story repeats itself. [20,9]

The market

The market process

In an occasional act of barter in which men who ordinarily do not resort to trading with other people exchange goods ordinarily not negotiated, the ratio of exchange is determined only within broad margins. Catallactics, the theory of exchange ratios and prices, cannot determine at what point within these margins the concrete ratio will be established. All that it can assert with regard to such exchanges is that they can be effected only if each party values what he receives more highly than what he gives away. [16,1]

The recurrence of individual acts of exchange generates the market step by step with the evolution of the division of labor within a society based on private property. As it becomes a rule to produce for other people's consumption, the members of society must sell and buy. The multiplication of the acts of exchange and the increase in the number of people offering or asking for the same commodities narrow the margins between the valuations of the parties. Indirect exchange and its perfection through the use of money divide the transactions into two different parts: sale and purchase. What in the eyes of one party is a sale, is for the other party a purchase. The divisibility of money, unlimited for all practical purposes, makes it possible to determine the exchange ratios with nicety. The exchange ratios are now as a rule money prices. They are determined between extremely narrow margins: the valuations on the one hand of the marginal buyer and those of the marginal offerer who abstains from selling, and the valuations on the other hand of the marginal seller and those of the marginal potential buyer who abstains from buying. [16,1]

The deal is always advantageous both for the buyer and the seller. Even a man who sells at a loss is still better off than he would be if he could not sell at all, or only at a still lower price. He loses on account of his lack of foresight; the sale limits his loss even if the price received is low. If both the buyer and the seller were not to consider the transaction as the most advantageous action they could choose under the prevailing conditions, they would not enter into the deal. [24,1]

When the baker provides the dentist with bread and the dentist relieves the baker's toothache, neither the baker nor the dentist is harmed. It is wrong to consider such an exchange of services and the pillage of the baker's shop by armed gangsters as two manifestations of the same thing. Foreign trade differs from domestic trade only in so far as goods and services are exchanged beyond the borderlines separating the territories of two sovereign nations. [24,1]

The market is not a place, a thing, or a collective entity. The market is a process, actuated by the interplay of the actions of the various individuals cooperating under the division of labor. The forces determining the – continually changing – state of the market are the value judgments of these individuals and their actions as directed by these value judgments. The state of the market at any instant is the price structure, i.e., the totality of the exchange ratios as established by the interaction of those eager to buy and those eager to sell. There is nothing inhuman or mystical with regard to the market. The market process is entirely a resultant of human actions. Every market phenomenon can be traced back to definite choices of the members of the market society. [15,1]

The market process is coherent and indivisible. It is an indissoluble intertwinement of actions and reactions, of moves and countermoves. But the insufficiency of our mental abilities enjoins upon us the necessity of dividing it into parts and analyzing each of these parts separately. In resorting to such artificial cleavages we must never forget that the seemingly autonomous existence of these parts is an imaginary makeshift of our minds. They are only parts, that is, they cannot even be thought of as existing outside the structure of which they are parts. [16,3]

There is in the operation of a market economy nothing which could properly be called distribution. Goods are not first produced and then distributed, as would be the case in a socialist state. [14,7 note]

The market process is the adjustment of the individual actions of the various members of the market society to the requirements of mutual cooperation. The market prices tell the producers what to produce, how to produce, and in what quantity. The market is the focal point to which the activities of the individuals converge. It is the center from which the activities of the individuals radiate. [15,1]

On the market agitation never stops. The imaginary construction of an evenly rotating economy has no counterpart in reality. There can never emerge a state of affairs in which the sum of the prices of the complementary factors of production, due allowance being made for time preference, equals the prices of the products and no further changes are to be expected. There are always profits to be earned by somebody. The speculators are always enticed by the expectation of profit. [16,1]

The imaginary construction of the evenly rotating economy is a mental tool for comprehension of entrepreneurial profit and loss. It is, to be sure, not a design for comprehension of the pricing process. The final prices corresponding to this imaginary conception are by no means identical with the market prices. The activities of the entrepreneurs or of any other actors on the economic scene are not guided by consideration of any such things as equilibrium prices and the evenly rotating economy. The entrepreneurs take into account anticipated future prices, not final prices or equilibrium prices. They discover discrepancies between the height of the prices of the complementary factors of production and the anticipated future prices of the products, and they are intent upon taking advantage of such discrepancies. These endeavors of the entrepreneurs would finally result in the emergence of the evenly rotating economy if no further changes in the data were to appear. [16,1]

The formation of prices

The ultimate source of the determination of prices is the value judgments of the consumers. Prices are the outcome of the valuation preferring a to b. They are social phenomena as they are brought about by the interplay of the valuations of all individuals participating in the operation of the market. Each individual, in buying or not buying and in selling or not selling, contributes his share to the formation of the market prices. But the larger the market is, the smaller is the weight of each individual's contribution. Thus the structure of market prices appears to the individual as a datum to which he must adjust his own conduct. [16,2]

The valuations which result in determination of definite prices are different. Each party attaches a higher value to the good he receives than to the good he gives away. The exchange ratio, the price, is not the product of an equality of valuation, but, on the contrary, the product of a discrepancy in valuation. [16,2]

The concept of a "just" or "fair" price is devoid of any scientific meaning; it is a disguise for wishes, a striving for a state of affairs different from reality. Market prices are entirely determined by the value judgments of men as they really act. [16,2]

If one says that prices tend toward a point at which total demand is equal to total supply, one resorts to another mode of expressing the same concatenation of phenomena. Demand and supply are the outcome of the conduct of those buying and selling. If, other things being equal, supply increases, prices must drop. At the previous price all those ready to pay this price could buy the quantity they wanted to buy. If the supply increases, they must buy larger quantities or other people who did not buy before must become interested in buying. This can only be attained at a lower price. [16,2]

The pricing process is a social process. It is consummated by an interaction of all members of the society. All collaborate and cooperate, each in the particular role he has chosen for himself in the framework of the division of labor. Competing in cooperation and cooperating in competition all people are instrumental in bringing about the result, viz., the price structure of the market, the allocation of the factors of production to the various lines of want-satisfaction, and the determination of the share of each individual. These three events are not three different matters. They are only different aspects of one indivisible phenomenon which our analytical scrutiny separates into three parts. In the market process they are accomplished uno actu. [16,3]

The economic process is a continuous interplay of production and consumption. Today's activities are linked with those of the past through the technological knowledge at hand, the amount and the quality of the capital goods among various individuals. They are linked with the future through the very essence of human action; action is always directed toward the improvement of future conditions. In order to see his way in the unknown and uncertain future man has within his reach only two aids: experience of past events and his faculty of understanding. Knowledge about past prices is a part of this experience and at the same time the starting point of understanding the future. [16,3]

Appraisement must be clearly distinguished from valuation. Appraisement in no way depends upon the subjective valuation of the man who appraises. He is not intent upon establishing the subjective use-value of the good concerned, but upon anticipating the prices which the market will determine. Valuation is a value judgment expressive of a difference in value. Appraisement is the anticipation of an expected fact. It aims at establishing what prices will be paid on the market for a particular commodity or what amount of money will be required for the purchase of a definite commodity. [16,2]

Valuation and appraisement are, however, closely connected. The valuations of an autarkic husbandman directly compare the weight he attaches to different means for the removal of uneasiness. The valuations of a man buying and selling on the market must not disregard the structure of market prices; they depend upon appraisement. In order to know the meaning of a price one must know the purchasing power of the amount of money concerned. It is necessary by and large to be familiar with the prices of those goods which one would like to acquire and to form on the ground of such knowledge an opinion about their future prices. If an individual speaks of the costs incurred by the purchase of some goods already acquired or to be incurred by the purchase of goods he plans to acquire, he expresses these costs in terms of money. But this amount of money represents in his eyes the degree of satisfaction he could obtain by employing it for the acquisition of other goods. The valuation makes a detour, it goes via the appraisement of the structure of market prices; but it always aims finally at the comparison of alternative modes for the removal of felt uneasiness. [16,2]

The market economy

The market economy is the social system of the division of labor under private ownership of the means of production. Everybody acts on his own behalf; but everybody's actions aim at the satisfaction of other people's needs as well as at the satisfaction of his own. Everybody in acting serves his fellow citizens. Everybody, on the other hand, is served by his fellow citizens. Everybody is both a means and an end in himself, an ultimate end for himself and a means to other people in their endeavors to attain their own ends. [15,1]

The market economy is a man-made mode of acting under the division of labor. But this does not imply that it is something accidental or artificial and could be replaced by another mode. The market economy is the product of a long evolutionary process. It is the outcome of man's endeavors to adjust his action in the best possible way to the given conditions of his environment that he cannot alter. It is the strategy, as it were, by the application of which man has triumphantly progressed from savagery to civilization. [15,3]

This system is steered by the market. The market directs the individual's activities into those channels in which he best serves the wants of his fellow men. There is in the operation of the market no compulsion and coercion. The state, the social apparatus of coercion and compulsion, does not interfere with the market and with the citizens' activities directed by the market. Each man is free; nobody is subject to a despot. Of his own accord the individual integrates himself into the cooperative system. The market directs him and reveals to him in what way he can best promote his own welfare as well as that of other people. The market is supreme. The market alone puts the whole social system in order and provides it with sense and meaning. [15,1]

No system of the social division of labor can do without a method that makes individuals responsible for their contributions to the joint productive effort. If this responsibility is not brought about by the price structure of the market and the inequality of wealth and income it begets, it must be enforced by the methods of direct compulsion as practiced by the police. [15,7]

The market economy must be strictly differentiated from the second thinkable – although not realizable – system of social cooperation under the division of labor; the system of social or governmental ownership of the means of production. This second system is commonly called socialism, communism, planned economy, or state capitalism. The market economy or capitalism, as it is usually called, and the socialist economy preclude one another. There is no mixture of the two systems possible or thinkable; there is no such thing as a mixed economy, a system that would be in part capitalist and in part socialist. Production is directed by the market or by the decrees of a production tsar or a committee of production tsars. [15,1]

It is customary to speak metaphorically of the automatic and anonymous forces actuating the "mechanism" of the market. In employing such metaphors people are ready to disregard the fact that the only factors directing the market and the determination of prices are purposive acts of men. There is no automatism; there are only men consciously and deliberately aiming at ends chosen. There are no mysterious mechanical forces; there is only the human will to remove uneasiness. There is no anonymity; there is I and you and Bill and Joe and all the rest. And each of us is both a producer and a consumer. [15,12]

The exchange relation is the fundamental social relation. Interpersonal exchange of goods and services weaves the bond which unites men into society. The societal formula is: *do ut des*. Where there is no intentional mutuality, where an action is performed without any design of being benefitted by a concomitant action of other men, there is no interpersonal exchange, but autistic exchange. It does not matter whether the autistic action is beneficial or detrimental to other people or whether it does not concern them at all. A genius may perform his task for himself, not for the crowd; however, he is an outstanding benefactor of mankind. The robber kills the victim for his own advantage; the murdered man is by no means a partner in this crime, he is merely its object; what is done, is done against him. [10,1]

The market is a social body; it is the foremost social body. The market phenomena are social phenomena. They are the resultant of each individual's active contribution. But they are different from each such contribution. They appear to the individual as something given which he himself cannot alter. He does not always see that he himself is a part, although a small part, of the complex of elements determining each momentary state of the market. Because he fails to realize this fact, he feels himself free, in criticizing the market phenomena, to condemn with regard to his fellow men a mode of conduct which he considers as quite right with regard to himself. He blames the market for its callousness and disregard of persons and asks for social control of the market in order to "humanize" it. He asks on the one hand for measures to protect the consumer against the producers. But on the other hand he insists even more passionately upon the necessity of protecting himself as a producer against the consumers. [15,12]

The entrepreneur

The driving force of the market process is provided neither by the consumers nor by the owners of the means of production – land, capital goods, and labor – but by the promoting and speculating entrepreneurs. These are people intent upon profiting by taking advantage of differences in prices. Quicker of apprehension and farther-sighted than other men, they look around for sources of profit. They buy where and when they deem prices too low, and they sell where and when they deem prices too high. They approach the owners of the factors of production, and their competition sends the prices of these factors up to the limit corresponding to their anticipation of the future prices of the products. They approach the consumers, and their competition forces prices of consumers' goods down to the point at which the whole supply can be sold. Profit-seeking speculation is the driving force of the market as it is the driving force of production. [16,1]

Living and acting man by necessity combines various functions. He is never merely a consumer. He is in addition either an entrepreneur, landowner, capitalist, or worker, or a person supported by the intake earned by such people. Moreover, the functions of the entrepreneur, the landowner, the capitalist, and the worker are very often combined in the same persons. History is intent upon classifying men according to the ends they aim at and the means they employ for the attainment of these ends. Economics, exploring the structure of acting in the market society without any regard to the ends people aim at and the means they employ, is intent upon discerning categories and functions. These are two different tasks. The difference can best be demonstrated in discussing the catallactic concept of the entrepreneur. [14,7]

The specific entrepreneurial function consists in determining the employment of the factors of production. The entrepreneur is the man who dedicates them to special purposes. In doing so he is driven solely by the selfish interest in making profits and in acquiring wealth. But he cannot evade the law of the market. He can succeed only by best serving the consumers. His profit depends on the approval of his conduct by the consumers. [15,8]

Economics, in speaking of entrepreneurs, has in view not men, but a definite function. This function is not the particular feature of a special group or class of men; it is inherent in every action and burdens every actor. In embodying this function in an imaginary figure, we resort to a methodological makeshift. The term entrepreneur as used by catallactic theory means: acting man exclusively seen from the aspect of the uncertainty inherent in every action. In using this term one must never forget that every action is embedded in the flux of time and therefore involves a speculation. The capitalists, the landowners, and the laborers are by necessity speculators. So is the consumer in providing for anticipated future needs. [14,7]

Let us try to think the imaginary construction of a pure entrepreneur to its ultimate logical consequences. This entrepreneur does not own any capital. The capital required for his entrepreneurial activities is lent to him by the capitalists in the form of money loans. The law, it is true, considers him the proprietor of the various means of production purchased by expending the sums borrowed. Nevertheless he remains propertyless as the amount of his assets is balanced by his liabilities. If he succeeds, the net profit is his. If he fails, the loss must fall upon the capitalists who have lent him the funds. Such an entrepreneur would, in fact, be an employee of the capitalists who speculates on their account and takes a 100 per cent share in the net profits without being concerned about the losses. But even if the entrepreneur is in a position to provide himself a part of the capital required and borrows only the rest, things are essentially not different. To the extent that the losses incurred cannot be borne out of the entrepreneur's own funds, they fall upon the lending capitalists, whatever the terms of the contract may be. A capitalist is always also virtually an entrepreneur and speculator. He always runs the chance of losing his funds. There is no such thing as a perfectly safe investment. [14,7]

The self-sufficient landowner who tills his estate only to supply his own household is affected by all changes influencing the fertility of his farm or his personal needs. Within a market economy the result of a farmer's activities is affected by all changes regarding the importance of his piece of land for supplying the market. The farmer is clearly, even from the point of view of mundane terminology, an entrepreneur. No proprietor of any means of production, whether they are represented in tangible goods or in money, remains untouched by the uncertainty of the future. The employment of any tangible goods or money for production, i.e., the provision for later days, is in itself an entrepreneurial activity. [14,7]

Things are essentially the same for the laborer. He is born the proprietor of certain abilities; his innate faculties are a means of production which is better fitted for some kinds of work, less fitted for others, and not at all fitted for still others. If he has acquired the skill needed for the performance of certain kinds of labor, he is, with regard to the time and the material outlays absorbed by this training in the position of an investor. He has made an input in the expectation of being compensated by an adequate output. The laborer is an entrepreneur in so far as his wages are determined by the price the market allows for the kind of work he can perform. This price varies according to the change in conditions in the same way in which the price of every other factor of production varies. [14,7]

In the context of economic theory the meaning of the terms concerned is this: Entrepreneur means acting man in regard to the changes occurring in the data of the market. Capitalist and landowner mean acting man in regard to the changes in value and price which, even with all the market data remaining equal, are brought about by the mere passing of time as a consequence of the different valuation of present goods and of future goods. Worker means man in regard to the employment of the factor of production human labor. Thus every function is nicely integrated: the entrepreneur earns profit or suffers loss; the owners of means of production (capital goods or land) earn originary interest; the workers earn wages. In this sense we elaborate the imaginary construction of functional distribution as different from the actual historical distribution. [14,7]

The sovereignty of the consumers

The direction of all economic affairs is in the market society a task of the entrepreneurs. Theirs is the control of production. They are at the helm and steer the ship. A superficial observer would believe that they are supreme. But they are not. They are bound to obey unconditionally the captain's orders. The captain is the consumer. Neither the entrepreneurs nor the farmers nor the capitalists determine what has to be produced. The consumers do that. If a businessman does not strictly obey the orders of the public as they are conveyed to him by the structure of market prices, he suffers losses, he goes bankrupt, and is thus removed from his eminent position at the helm. Other men who did better in satisfying the demand of the consumers replace him. [15,4]

The consumers patronize those shops in which they can buy what they want at the cheapest price. Their buying and their abstention from buying decides who should own and run the plants and the farms. They make poor people rich and rich people poor. They determine precisely what should be produced, in what quality, and in what quantities. [15,4]

Only the sellers of goods and services of the first order are in direct contact with the consumers and directly depend on their orders. But they transmit the orders received from the public to all those producing goods and services of the higher orders. For the manufacturers of consumers' goods, the retailers, the service trades, and the professions are forced to acquire what they need for the conduct of their own business from those purveyors who offer them at the cheapest price. If they were not intent upon buying in the cheapest market and arranging their processing of the factors of production so as to fill the demands of the consumers in the best and cheapest way, they would be forced to go out of business. More efficient men who succeeded better in buying and processing the factors of production would supplant them. [15,4]

The consumer is in a position to give free rein to his caprices and fancies. The entrepreneurs, capitalists, and farmers have their hands tied; they are bound to comply in their operations with the orders of the buying public. Every deviation from the lines prescribed by the demand of the consumers debits their account. The slightest deviation, whether willfully brought about or caused by error, bad judgment, or inefficiency, restricts their profits or makes them disappear. A more serious deviation results in losses and thus impairs or entirely absorbs their wealth. Capitalists, entrepreneurs, and landowners can only preserve and increase their wealth by filling best the orders of the consumers. They are not free to spend money which the consumers are not prepared to refund to them in paying more for the products. In the conduct of their business affairs they must be unfeeling and stony-hearted because the consumers, their bosses, are themselves unfeeling and stony-hearted. [15,4]

The consumers determine ultimately not only the prices of the consumers' goods, but no less the prices of all factors of production. They determine the income of every member of the market economy. The consumers, not the entrepreneurs, pay ultimately the wages earned by every worker, the glamorous movie star as well as the charwoman. With every penny spent the consumers determine the direction of all production processes and the details of the organization of all business activities. This state of affairs has been described by calling the market a democracy in which every penny gives a right to cast a ballot. It would be more correct to say that a democratic constitution is a scheme to assign to the citizens in the conduct of government the same supremacy the market economy gives them in their capacity as consumers. However, the comparison is imperfect. In the political democracy only the votes cast for the majority candidate or the majority plan are effective in shaping the course of affairs. The votes polled by the minority do not directly influence policies. But on the market no vote is cast in vain. Every penny spent has the power to work upon the production processes. The publishers cater not only to the majority by publishing detective stories, but also to the minority reading lyrical poetry and philosophical tracts. The bakeries bake bread not only for healthy people, but also for the sick on special diets. The decision of a consumer is carried into effect with the full momentum he gives it through his readiness to spend a definite amount of money. [15,4]

It is true, in the market the various consumers have not the same voting right. The rich cast more votes than the poorer citizens. But this inequality is itself the outcome of a previous voting process. To be rich, in a pure market economy, is the outcome of success in filling best the demands of the consumers. A wealthy man can preserve his wealth only by continuing to serve the consumers in the most efficient way. [15,4]

Thus the owners of the material factors of production and the entrepreneurs are virtually mandataries or trustees of

the consumers, revocably appointed by an election daily repeated. [15,4]

The prices of the factors of production

The market determines prices of factors of production
in the same way in which it determines prices of consumers'
goods. The market process is an interaction of men deliberately
striving after the best possible removal of dissatisfaction. It is
impossible to think away or to eliminate from the market process the men actuating its operation. One cannot deal with the
market of consumers' goods and disregard the actions of the
consumers. One cannot deal with the market of the goods of
higher orders while disregarding the actions of the entrepreneurs and the fact that the use of money is essential in their
transactions. There is nothing automatic or mechanical in the
operation of the market. The entrepreneurs, eager to earn
profits, appear as bidders at an auction, as it were, in which the
owners of the factors of production put up for sale land, capital goods, and labor. The entrepreneurs are eager to outdo one
another by bidding higher prices than their rivals. Their offers
are limited on the one hand by their anticipation of future
prices of the products and on the other hand by the necessity
to snatch the factors of production away from the hands of
other entrepreneurs competing with them. [16,3]

The entrepreneur is the agency that prevents the persistence of a state of production unsuitable to fill the most urgent
wants of the consumers in the cheapest way. All people are
anxious for the best possible satisfaction of their wants and are
in this sense striving after the highest profit they can reap. The
mentality of the promoters, speculators, and entrepreneurs is
not different from that of their fellow men. They are merely
superior to the masses in mental power and energy. They are
the leaders on the way toward material progress. They are the
first to understand that there is a discrepancy between what is
done and what could be done. They guess what the consumers
would like to have and are intent upon providing them with
these things. In the pursuit of such plans they bid higher prices
for some factors of production and lower the prices of other
factors of production by restricting their demand for them. In

supplying the market with those consumers' goods in the sale
of which the highest profits can be earned, they create a tendency toward a fall in their prices. In restricting the output of
those consumers' goods the production of which does not offer chances for reaping profit, they bring about a tendency toward a rise in their prices. All these transformations go on
ceaselessly and could stop only if the unrealizable conditions of
the evenly rotating economy and of static equilibrium were to
be attained. [16,3]

In drafting their plans the entrepreneurs look first at the
prices of the immediate past which are mistakenly called
present prices. Of course, the entrepreneurs never make these
prices enter into their calculations without paying regard to anticipated changes. The prices of the immediate past are for
them only the starting point of deliberations leading to forecasts of future prices. The prices of the past do not influence
the determination of future prices. It is, on the contrary, the
anticipation of future prices of the products that determines
the state of prices of the complementary factors of production.
The determination of prices has, as far as the mutual exchange
ratios between various commodities are concerned, no direct
causal relation whatever with the prices of the past. [16,3]

Each entrepreneur represents a different aspect of the
consumers' wants, either a different commodity or another way
of producing the same commodity. The competition among
the entrepreneurs is ultimately a competition among the various possibilities open to men to remove their uneasiness as far
as possible by the acquisition of consumers' goods. The decisions of the consumers to buy one commodity and to postpone buying another determine the prices of factors of production required for manufacturing these commodities. The competition between the entrepreneurs reflects the prices of consumers' goods in the formation of the prices of the factors of
production. It reflects in the external world the conflict which
the inexorable scarcity of the factors of production brings
about in the soul of each individual. It makes effective the sub-
sumed decisions of the consumers as to what purpose the nonspecific factors should be used for and to what extent the specific factors of production should be used. [16,3]

The operation of the entrepreneurs brings about a tendency toward an equalization of prices for the same goods in all subdivisions of the market, due allowance being made for the cost of transportation and the time absorbed by it. Differences in prices which are not merely transitory and bound to be wiped out by entrepreneurial action are always the outcome of particular obstacles obstructing the inherent tendency toward equalization. [16,1]

Entrepreneurial profit and loss

In the market economy all those things that are bought and sold against money are marked with money prices. In the monetary calculus profit appears as a surplus of money received over money expended and loss as a surplus of money expended over money received. Profit and loss can be expressed in definite amounts of money. It is possible to ascertain in terms of money how much an individual has profited or lost. However, this is not a a statement about this individual's psychic profit or loss. It is a statement about a social phenomenon, about the individual's contribution to the societal effort as it is appraised by the other members of society. It does not tell us anything about the individual's increase or decrease in satisfaction or happiness. It merely reflects his fellow men's evaluation of his contribution to social cooperation. This evaluation is ultimately determined by the efforts of every member of society to attain the highest possible psychic profit. It is the resultant of the composite effect of all these people's subjective and personal value judgments as manifested in their conduct on the market. But it must not be confused with these value judgments as such. [15,8]

Like every acting man, the entrepreneur is always a speculator. He deals with the uncertain conditions of the future. His success or failure depends on the correctness of his anticipation of uncertain events. If he fails in his understanding of things to come, he is doomed. The only source from which an entrepreneur's profits stem is his ability to anticipate better than other people the future demand of the consumers. [15,8]

If all entrepreneurs were to anticipate correctly the future state of the market, there would be neither profits nor losses. The prices of all the factors of production would already today be fully adjusted to tomorrow's prices of the products. In buying the factors of production the entrepreneur would have to expend (with due allowance for the difference between the prices of present goods and future goods) no less an amount than the buyers will pay him later for the product. An entrepreneur can make a profit only if he anticipates future conditions more correctly than other entrepreneurs. Then he buys the complementary factors of production at prices the sum of which, including allowance for the time difference, is smaller than the price at which he sells the product. [15,8]

One must not confuse entrepreneurial profit and loss with other factors affecting the entrepreneur's proceeds. [15,8]

The entrepreneur's technological ability does not affect the specific entrepreneurial profit or loss. As far as his own technological activities contribute to the returns earned and increase his net income, we are confronted with a compensation for work rendered. It is wages paid to the entrepreneur for his labor. [15,8]

What produces a man's profit in the course of affairs within an unhampered market society is not his fellow citizen's plight and distress, but the fact that he alleviates or entirely removes what causes his fellow citizen's feeling of uneasiness. What hurts the sick is the plague, not the physician who treats the disease. The doctor's gain is not an outcome of the epidemics, but of the aid he gives to those affected. The ultimate source of profits is always the foresight of future conditions. Those who succeeded better than others in anticipating future events and in adjusting their activities to the future state of the market, reap profits because they are in a position to satisfy the most urgent needs of the public. The profits of those who have produced goods and services for which the buyers scramble are not the source of the losses of those who have brought to the market commodities in the purchase of which the public is not prepared to pay the full amount of production costs expended. These losses are caused by the lack of insight displayed in anticipating the future state of the market and the demand of the consumers. [24,1]

It is wrong to look at these problems from the point of view of resentment and envy. It is no less faulty to restrict one's observation to the momentary position of various individuals. These are social problems and must be judged with regard to the operation of the whole market system. What secures the best possible satisfaction of the demands of each member of society is precisely the fact that those who succeeded better than other people in anticipating future conditions are earning profits. [24,1]

Competition

In nature there prevail irreconcilable conflicts of interests. The means of subsistence are scarce. Proliferation tends to outrun subsistence. Only the fittest plants and animals survive. The antagonism between an animal starving to death and another that snatches the food away from it is implacable. [15,5]

Social cooperation under the division of labor removes such antagonisms. It substitutes partnership and mutuality for hostility. The members of society are united in a common venture. [15,5]

Catallactic competition is emulation between people who want to surpass one another. It is not a fight, although it is usual to apply to it in a metaphorical sense the terminology of war and internecine conflict, of attack and defense, of strategy and tactics. Those who fail are not annihilated; they are removed to a place in the social system that is more modest, but more adequate to their achievements than that which they had planned to attain. [15,5]

As far as natural conditions come into play, competition can only be "free" with regard to those factors of production which are not scarce and therefore not objects of human action. In the catallactic field competition is always restricted by the inexorable scarcity of the economic goods and services. Even in the absence of institutional barriers erected to restrict the number of those competing, the state of affairs is never such as to enable everyone to compete in all sectors of the market. In each sector only comparatively small groups can engage in competition. [15,5]

Catallactic competition, one of the characteristic features of the market economy, is a social phenomenon. It is not a right, guaranteed by the state and the laws, that would make it possible for every individual to choose ad libitum the place in the structure of the division of labor he likes best. To assign to everybody his proper place in society is the task of the consumers. Their buying and abstention from buying is instrumental in determining each individual's social position. Their supremacy is not impaired by any privileges granted to the individuals qua producers. Entrance into a definite branch of industry is virtually free to newcomers only as far as the consumers approve of this branch's expansion or as far as the newcomers succeed in supplanting those already occupied in it by filling better or more cheaply the demands of the consumers. Additional investment is reasonable only to the extent that it fills the most urgent among the not yet satisfied needs of the consumers. If the existing plants are sufficient, it would be wasteful to invest more capital in the same industry. The structure of market prices pushes the new investors into other branches. [15,5]

The selective process of the market is actuated by the composite effort of all members of the market economy. Driven by the urge to remove his own uneasiness as much as possible, each individual is intent, on the one hand, upon attaining that position in which he can contribute most to the best satisfaction of everyone else and, on the other hand, upon taking best advantage of the services offered by everyone else. This means that he tries to sell on the dearest market and to buy on the cheapest market. The resultant of these endeavors is not only the price structure but no less the social structure, the assignment of definite tasks to the various individuals. The market makes people rich or poor, determines who shall run the big plants and who shall scrub the floors, fixes how many people shall work in the copper mines and how many in the symphony orchestras. None of these decisions is made once and for all; they are revocable every day. The selective process never stops. It goes on adjusting the social apparatus of production to the changes in demand and supply. It reviews again and again its previous decisions and forces everybody to submit to a new examination of his case. There is no security and no such thing as a right to preserve any position acquired in the past. Nobody is exempt from the law of the market, the consumers' sovereignty. [15,11]

Ownership of the means of production is not a privilege, but a social liability. Capitalists and landowners are compelled to employ their property for the best possible satisfaction of the consumers. If they are slow and inept in the performance of their duties, they are penalized by losses. If they do not learn the lesson and do not reform their conduct of affairs, they lose their wealth. No investment is safe forever. He who does not use his property in serving the consumers in the most efficient way is doomed to failure. There is no room left for people who would like to enjoy their fortunes in idleness and thoughtlessness. The proprietor must aim to invest his funds in such a way that principal and yield are at least not impaired. [15,11]

The point of view from which the consumers choose the captains of industry and business is exclusively their qualification to adjust production to the needs of the consumers. They do not bother about other features and merits. They want a shoe manufacturer to fabricate good and cheap shoes. They are not intent upon entrusting the conduct of the shoe trade to handsome amiable boys, to people of good drawing-room manners, of artistic gifts, of scholarly habits, or of any other virtues or talents. A proficient businessman may often be deficient in many accomplishments which contribute to the success of a man in other spheres of life. [15,11]

It is an old fallacy that it is a legitimate task of civil government to protect the less efficient producer against the competition of the more efficient. One asks for a "producers' policy: as distinct from a "consumers' policy." While flamboyantly repeating the truism that the only aim of production is to provide ample supplies for consumption, people emphasize with no less eloquence that the "industrious" producer should be protected against the "idle" consumer. [15,12]

However, producers and consumers are identical. Production and consumption are different stages in acting. Catallactics embodies these differences in speaking of producers and consumers. But in reality they are the same people. It is, of course, possible to protect a less efficient producer against the competition of more efficient fellows. Such a privilege conveys to the privileged the benefits which the unhampered market provides only to those who succeed in best filling the wants of the consumers. But it necessarily impairs the satisfaction of the consumers. If only one producer or a small group is privileged, the beneficiaries enjoy an advantage at the expense of the rest of the people. But if all producers are privileged to the same extent, everybody loses in his capacity as consumer as much as he gains in his capacity as a producer. Moreover, all are injured because the supply of products drops if the most efficient men are prevented from employing their skill in that field in which they could render the best services to the consumers. [15,12]

Private property

Private ownership of the means of production is the fundamental institution of the market economy. It is the institution the presence of which characterizes the market economy as such. Where it is absent, there is no question of a market economy. [24,4]

In dealing with private property, catallactics deals with control, not with legal terms, concepts and definitions. Private ownership means that the proprietors determine the employment of the factors of production, while public ownership means that the government controls their employment. [24,4]

Private property is a human device. It is not sacred. It came into existence in early ages of history, when people with their own power and by their own authority appropriated to themselves what had previously not been anybody's property. Again and again proprietors were robbed of their property by expropriation. The history of private property can be traced back to a point at which it originated out of acts which were certainly not legal. Virtually every owner is the direct or indirect legal successor of people who acquired ownership either by arbitrary appropriation of ownerless things or by violent spoliation of their predecessor. [24,4]

However, the fact that legal formalism can trace back every title either to arbitrary appropriation or to violent expropriation has no significance whatever for the conditions of a market society. Ownership in the market economy is no longer linked up with the remote origin of private property. Those events in a far-distant past, hidden in the darkness of primitive mankind's history, are no longer of any concern for our day. For in an unhampered market society the consumers daily decide anew who should own and how much he should own. The consumers allot control of the means of production to those who know how to use them best for the satisfaction of the most urgent wants of the consumers. Only in a legal and formalistic sense can the owners be considered the successors of appropriators and expropriators. In fact, they are mandataries of the consumers, bound by the operation of the market to serve the consumers best. Under capitalism, private property is the consummation of the self-determination of the consumers. [24,4]

In the market society the proprietors of capital and land can enjoy their property only by employing it for the satisfaction of other people's wants. They must serve the consumers in order to have any advantage from what is their own. The very fact that they own means of production forces them to submit to the wishes of the public. Ownership is an asset only for those who know how to employ it in the best possible way for the benefit of the consumers. It is a social function. [24,4]

It is customary nowadays to signify the position which the owners of property and the entrepreneurs occupy on the market as economic power or market power. This terminology is misleading when applied to the conditions of the market. All that happens in the unhampered market economy is controlled by the laws dealt with by catallactics. All market phenomena are ultimately determined by the choices of the consumers. If one wants to apply the notion of power to phenomena of the market, one ought to say: in the market all power is vested in the consumers. The entrepreneurs are forced, by the necessity of earning profits and avoiding losses, to consider in every re-

gard – e.g. also in the conduct of the wrongly so-called "internal" affairs of their plants, especially personnel management
– the best possible and cheapest satisfaction of the consumers
as their supreme directive. It is very inexpedient to employ the
same term "power" in dealing with a firm's ability to supply the
consumers with automobiles, shoes, or margarine better than
others do and in referring to the strength of a government's
armed forces to crush any resistance. [23,2]

Ownership of material factors of production as well as
entrepreneurial or technological skill do not – in the market
economy – bestow power in the coercive sense. All they grant
is the privilege to serve the real masters of the market, the consumers, in a more exalted position than other people. Ownership of capital is a mandate entrusted to the owners, under the
condition that it should be employed for the best possible satisfaction of the consumers. He who does not comply with this
imposition forfeits his wealth and is relegated to a place in
which his ineptitude no longer hurts people's well-being. [23,2]

External costs and external economies

Carried through consistently, the right of property would
entitle the proprietor to claim all the advantages which the
good's employment may generate on the one hand and would
burden him with all the disadvantages resulting from its employment on the other hand. Then the proprietor alone would
be fully responsible for the outcome. In dealing with his property he would take into account all the expected results of his
action, those considered favorable as well as those considered
unfavorable. But if some of the consequences of his action are
outside of the sphere of the benefits he is entitled to reap and
of the drawbacks that are put to his debit, he will not bother in
his planning about all the effects of his action. He will disregard those benefits which do not increase his own satisfaction
and those costs which do not burden him. His conduct will de-
viate from the line which it would have followed if the laws
were better adjusted to the economic objectives of private
ownership. He will embark upon certain projects only because
the laws release him from responsibility for some of the costs
incurred. He will abstain from other projects merely because

the laws prevent him from harvesting all the advantages deriv-
able. [23,6]

Whether the proprietor's relief from responsibility for
some of the disadvantages resulting from his conduct of affairs
is the outcome of a deliberate policy on the part of governments and legislators or whether it is an unintentional effect of
the traditional wording of laws, it is at any rate a datum which
the actors must take into account. They are faced with the
problem of external costs. Then some people choose certain
modes of want-satisfaction merely on account of the fact that a
part of the costs incurred are debited not to them but to other
people. [23,6]

If land is not owned by anybody, although legal formalism may call it public property, it is utilized without any regard
to the disadvantages resulting. Those who are in a position to
appropriate to themselves the returns – lumber and game of
the forests, fish of the water areas, and mineral deposits of the
subsoil – do not bother about the later effects of their mode of
exploitation. For them the erosion of the soil, the depletion of
the exhaustible resources and other impairments of the future
utilization are external costs not entering into their calculation
of input and output. They cut down the trees without any regard for fresh shoots or reforestation. In hunting and fishing
they do not shrink from methods preventing the repopulation
of the hunting and fishing grounds. [23,6]

It is true that where a considerable part of the costs incurred are external costs from the point of view of the acting
individuals or firms, the economic calculation established by
them is manifestly defective and their results deceptive. But
this is not the outcome of alleged deficiencies inherent in the
system of private ownership of the means of production. It is
on the contrary a consequence of loopholes left in this system.
It could be removed by a reform of the laws concerning liability for damages inflicted and by rescinding the institutional barriers preventing the full operation of private ownership. [23,6]

The case of external economies is not simply the inver-
sion of the case of external costs. It has its own domain and
character. If the results of an actor's action benefit not only

himself, but also other people, two alternatives are possible: [23,6]

1. The planning actor considers the advantages which he expects for himself so important that he is prepared to defray all the costs required. The fact that his project also benefits other people will not prevent him from accomplishing what promotes his own well-being. When a railroad company erects dikes to protect its tracks against snowslides and avalanches, it also protects the houses on adjacent grounds. But the benefits which its neighbors will derive will not hinder the company from embarking upon an expenditure that it deems expedient. [23,6]

2. The costs incurred by a project are so great that none of those whom it will benefit is ready to expend them in full. The project can be realized only if a sufficient number of those interested in it share in the costs. [23,6]

A project P is unprofitable when and because consumers prefer the satisfaction expected from the realization of some other projects to the satisfaction expected from the realization of P. The realization of P would withdraw capital and labor from the realization of some other projects for which the demand of the consumers is more urgent. The layman and the pseudo-economist fail to recognize this fact. They stubbornly refuse to notice the scarcity of the factors of production. [23,6]

Wages

Labor is a scarce factor of production. As such it is sold and bought on the market. The price paid for labor is included in the price allowed for the product or the services if the performer of the work is the seller of the product or the services. If bare labor is sold and bought as such, either by an entrepreneur engaged in production for sale or by a consumer eager to use the services rendered for his own consumption, the price paid is called wages. [21,3]

For acting man his own labor is not merely a factor of production but also the source of disutility; he values it not only with regard to the mediate gratification expected but also with regard to the disutility it causes. But for him, as for everyone, other people's labor as offered for sale on the market is nothing but a factor of production. Man deals with other people's labor in the same way that he deals with all scarce material factors of production. He appraises it according to the principles he applies in the appraisal of all other goods. The height of wage rates is determined on the market in the same way in which the prices of all commodities are determined. In this sense we may say that labor is a commodity. [21,3]

A uniform type of labor or a general rate of wages do not exist. Labor is very different in quality, and each kind of labor renders specific services. Each is appraised as a complementary factor for turning out definite consumers' goods and services. Between the appraisal of the performance of a surgeon and that of a stevedore there is no direct connection. But indirectly each sector of the labor market is connected with all other sectors. An increase in the demand for surgical services, however great, will not make stevedores flock into the practice of surgery. Yet the lines between the various sectors of the labor market are not sharply drawn. There prevails a continuous tendency for workers to shift from their branch to other similar occupations in which conditions seem to offer better opportunities. Thus finally every change in demand or supply in one sector affects all other sectors indirectly. [21,3]

Connexity exists not only between different types of labor and the prices paid for them but no less between labor and the material factors of production. Within certain limits labor can be substituted for material factors of production and vice versa. The extent that such substitutions are resorted to depends on the height of wage rates and the prices of material factors. [21,3]

The determination of wage rates – like that of the prices of material factors of production – can be achieved only on the market. There is no such thing as nonmarket wage rates, just as there are no nonmarket prices. As far as there are wages, labor is dealt with like any material factor of production and sold and bought on the market. It is usual to call the sector of the market of producers' goods on which labor is hired the labor market. [21,3]

As with all other sectors of the market, the labor market is actuated by the entrepreneurs intent upon making profits. Each entrepreneur is eager to buy all the kinds of specific labor he needs for the realization of his plans at the cheapest price. But the wages he offers must be high enough to take the workers away from competing entrepreneurs. The upper limit of his bidding is determined by anticipation of the price he can obtain for the increment in salable goods he expects from the employment of the worker concerned. The lower limit is determined by the bids of competing entrepreneurs who themselves are guided by analogous considerations. It is this that economists have in mind in asserting that the height of wage rates for each kind of labor is determined by its marginal productivity. Another way to express the same truth is to say that wage rates are determined by the supply of labor and of material factors of production on the one hand and by the anticipated future prices of the consumers' goods. [21,3]

The entrepreneurs are in the same position with regard to the sellers of labor as they are with regard to the sellers of the material factors of production. They are under the necessity of acquiring all factors of production at the cheapest price. But if in the pursuit of this endeavor some entrepreneurs, certain groups of entrepreneurs, or all entrepreneurs offer prices or wage rates which are too low, i.e., do not agree with the state of the unhampered market, they will succeed in acquiring what they want to acquire only if entrance into the ranks of entrepreneurship is blocked through institutional barriers. If the emergence of new entrepreneurs or the expansion of the activities of already operating entrepreneurs is not prevented, any drop in the prices of factors of production not consonant with the structure of the market must open new chances for the earning of profits. There will be people eager to take advantage of the margin between the prevailing wage rate and the marginal productivity of labor. Their demand for labor will bring wage rates back to the height conditioned by labor's marginal productivity. The tacit combination among the employers to which Adam Smith referred, even if it existed, could not lower wages below the competitive market rate unless access to entrepreneurship required not only brains and capital (the latter always available to enterprises promising the highest returns), but in addition also an institutional title, a patent, or a license, reserved to a class of privileged people. [21,3]

Wages and subsistence

The life of primitive man was an unceasing struggle against the scantiness of the nature-given means for his sustenance. In this desperate effort to secure bare survival, many individuals and whole families, tribes, and races succumbed. Primitive man was always haunted by the specter of death from starvation. Civilization has freed us from these perils. Human life is menaced day and night by innumerable dangers; it can be destroyed at any instant by natural forces which are beyond control or at least cannot be controlled at the present stage of our knowledge and our potentialities. But the horror of starvation no longer terrifies people living in a capitalist society. He who is able to work earns much more than is needed for bare sustenance. [21,6]

In the capitalist society there prevails a tendency toward a steady increase in the per capita quota of capital invested. The accumulation of capital soars above the increase in population figures. Consequently the marginal productivity of labor, real wage rates, and the wage earners' standard of living tend to rise continually. But this improvement in well-being is not the manifestation of the operation of an inevitable law of human evolution; it is a tendency resulting from the interplay of forces which can freely produce their effects only under capitalism. [21,6]

It is true, wage earners are imbued with the idea that wages must be at least high enough to enable them to maintain a standard of living adequate to their station in the hierarchical gradation of society. Every single worker has his particular opinion about the claims he is entitled to raise on account of "status," "rank," "tradition," and "custom" in the same way as he has his particular opinion about his own efficiency and his own achievements. But such pretensions and self-complacent assumptions are without any relevance for the determination of wage rates. They limit neither the upward nor the downward

movement of wage rates. The wage earner must sometimes satisfy himself with much less than what, according to his opinion, is adequate to his rank and efficiency. If he is offered more
than he expected, he pockets the surplus without a qualm.
[21,6]

What initiates the chain of actions that results in an improvement of economic conditions is the accumulation of new
capital through saving. These additional funds render the execution of projects possible which, for the lack of capital goods,
could not have been executed previously. Embarking upon the
realization of the new projects, the entrepreneurs compete on
the market for the factors of production with all those already
engaged in projects previously entered upon. In their attempts
to secure the necessary quantity of raw materials and of manpower, they push up the prices of raw materials and wage rates.
Thus the wage earners, already at the start of the process, reap
a share of the benefits that the abstention from consumption
on the part of the savers has begotten. In the farther course of
the process they are again favored, now in their capacity as
consumers, by the drop in prices that the increase in production tends to bring about. [21,6]

Economics describes the final outcome of this sequence
of changes thus: An increase in capital invested results, with an
unchanged number of people intent upon earning wages, in a
rise of the marginal utility of labor and therefore of wage rates.
What raises wage rates is an increase in capital exceeding the
increase in population or, in other words, an increase in the
per-head quota of capital invested. On the unhampered labor
market, wage rates always tend toward the height at which they
equal the marginal productivity of each kind of labor, that is
the height that equals the value added to or subtracted from
the value of the product by the employment or discharge of a
man. At this rate all those in search of employment find jobs,
and all those eager to employ workers can hire as many as they
want. If wages are raised above this market rate, unemploy-
ment of a part of the potential labor force inevitably results.
[21,6]

Wage rates are ultimately determined by the value which
the wage earner's fellow citizens attach to his services and

achievements. Labor is appraised like a commodity, not because the entrepreneurs and capitalists are hardhearted and cal-
lous, but because they are unconditionally subject to the
supremacy of the consumers of which today the earners of
wages and salaries form the immense majority. The consumers
are not prepared to satisfy anybody's pretensions, presump-
tions, and self-conceit. They want to be served in the cheapest
way. [21,6]

The labor market

Wages are the prices paid for the factor of production,
human labor. As is the case with all the other prices of complementary factors of production their height is ultimately determined by the prices of the products as they are expected at the
instant the labor is sold and bought. It does not matter
whether he who performs the labor sells his services to an employer who combines them with the material factors production and with the services of other people or whether he himself embarks upon his own account and peril upon these acts
of combination. The final price of labor of the same quality is
at any rate the same in the whole market system. [21,9]

In the changing economy there prevails a tendency for market
wage rates to adjust themselves precisely to the state of the final wage rates. This adjustment is a time-absorbing process.
The length of the period of adjustment depends on the time
required for the training for new jobs and for the removal of
workers to new places of residence. It depends furthermore on
subjective factors, as for instance the workers' familiarity with
the conditions and prospects of the labor market. The adjustment is a speculative venture as far as the training for new jobs
and the change of residence involve costs which are expended
only if one believes that the future state of the labor market
will make them appear profitable. [21,9]

With regard to all these things there is nothing that is
peculiar to labor, wages, and the labor market. What gives a
particular feature to the labor market is that the worker is not
merely the purveyor of the factor of production labor, but also

a human being and that it is impossible to sever the man from
his performance. [21,9]

Society and government

Human cooperation

Society is concerted action, cooperation. Society is the outcome of conscious and purposeful behavior. [8,1]

This does not mean that individuals have concluded contracts by virtue of which they have founded human society. The actions which have brought about social cooperation and daily bring it about anew do not aim at anything else than cooperation and coadjuvancy with others for the attainment of definite singular ends. The total complex of the mutual relations created by such concerted actions is called society. It substitutes collaboration for the – at least conceivable – isolated life of individuals. Society is division of labor and combination of labor. In his capacity as an acting animal man becomes a social animal. [8,1]

Individual man is born into a socially organized environment. In this sense alone we may accept the saying that society is – logically or historically – antecedent to the individual. In every other sense this dictum is either empty or nonsensical. The individual lives and acts within society. But society is nothing but the combination of individuals for cooperative effort. It exists nowhere else than in the actions of individual men. It is a delusion to search for it outside the actions of individuals. To speak of a society's autonomous and independent existence, of its life, its soul, and its actions is a metaphor which can easily lead to crass errors. [8,1]

The questions whether society or the individual is to be considered as the ultimate end, and whether the interests of society should be subordinated to those of the individuals or the interests of the individuals to those of society are fruitless. Action is always action of individual men. The social or societal element is a certain orientation of the actions of individual men. The category end makes sense only when applied to action. [8,1]

The fundamental facts that brought about cooperation, society, and civilization and transformed the animal man into a human being are the facts that work performed under the division of labor is more productive than isolated work and that man's reason is capable of recognizing this truth. But for these facts men would have forever remained deadly foes of one another, irreconcilable rivals in their endeavors to secure a portion of the scarce supply of means of sustenance provided by nature. Each man would have been forced to view all other men as his enemies; his craving for the satisfaction of his own appetites would have brought him into an implacable conflict with all his neighbors. No sympathy could possibly develop under such a state of affairs. [8,1]

Society is not merely interaction. There is interaction – reciprocal influence – between all parts of the universe: between the wolf and the sheep he devours; between the germ and the man it kills; between the falling stone and the thing upon which it falls. Society, on the other hand, always involves men acting in cooperation with other men in order to let all participants attain their own ends. [8,7]

The individual within society

If praxeology speaks of the solitary individual, acting on his own behalf only and independent of fellow men, it does so for the sake of a better comprehension of the problems of social cooperation. We do not assert that such isolated autarkic human beings have ever lived and that the social stage of man's nonhuman ancestors and the emergence of the primitive social bonds were effected in the same process. Man appeared on the scene of earthly events as a social being. The isolated asocial man is a fictitious construction. [8,6]

Seen from the point of view of the individual, society is the great means for the attainment of all his ends. The preservation of society is an essential condition of any plans an individual may want to realize by any action whatever. Even the refractory delinquent who fails to adjust his conduct to the requirements of life within the societal system of cooperation does not want to miss any of the advantages derived from the division of labor. He does not consciously aim at the destruction of society. He wants to lay his hands on a greater portion of the jointly produced wealth than the social order assigns to him. He would feel miserable if antisocial behavior were to become universal and its inevitable outcome, the return to primitive indigence, resulted. [8,6]

It is illusory to maintain that individuals in renouncing the alleged blessings of a fabulous state of nature and entering into society have foregone some advantages and have a fair claim to be indemnified for what they have lost. The idea that anybody would have fared better under an asocial state of mankind and is wronged by the very existence of society is absurd. Thanks to the higher productivity of social cooperation the human species has multiplied far beyond the margin of subsistence offered by the conditions prevailing in ages with a rudimentary degree of the division of labor. Each man enjoys a standard of living much higher than that of his savage ancestors. The natural condition of man is extreme poverty and insecurity. It is romantic nonsense to lament the passing of the happy days of primitive barbarism. In a state of savagery the complainants would either not have reached the age of manhood, or if they had, they would have lacked the opportunities and amenities provided by civilization. [8,6]

What makes friendly relations between human beings possible is the higher productivity of the division of labor. It removes the natural conflict of interests. For where there is division of labor, there is no longer question of the distribution of a supply not capable of enlargement. Thanks to the higher productivity of labor performed under the division of tasks, the supply of goods multiplies. A pre-eminent common interest, the preservation and further intensification of social cooperation, becomes paramount and obliterates all essential collisions. Catallactic competition is substituted for biological competition. It makes for harmony of the interests of all members of society. [24,3]

The very condition from which the irreconcilable conflicts of biological competition arise – viz., the fact that all people by and large strive after the same things – is transformed into a factor making for harmony of interests. Because many people or even all people want bread, clothes, shoes, and cars, large-scale production of these goods becomes feasible and reduces the costs of production to such an extent that they are accessible at low prices. The fact that my fellow man wants to acquire shoes as I do, does not make it harder for me to get shoes, but easier. What enhances the price of shoes is the fact that nature does not provide a more ample supply of leather and other raw material required, and that one must submit to the disutility of labor in order to transform these raw materials into shoes. The catallactic competition of those who, like me, are eager to have shoes makes shoes cheaper, not more expensive. [24,3]

The fact that not all human wants can be satisfied is not due to inappropriate social institutions or to deficiencies of the system of the market economy. It is a natural condition of human life. The belief that nature bestows upon man inexhaustible riches and that misery is an outgrowth of man's failure to organize the good society is entirely fallacious. The "state of nature" which the reformers and utopians depicted as paradisiac was in fact a state of extreme poverty and distress. "Poverty," says Bentham, "is not the work of the laws, it is the primitive condition of the human race." Even those at the base of the social pyramid are much better off than they would have been in the absence of social cooperation. They too are benefitted by the operation of the market economy and participate in the advantages of civilized society. [24,3]

There are two different kinds of social cooperation: cooperation by virtue of contract and coordination, and cooperation by virtue of command and subordination or hegemony. [10,2]

Where and as far as cooperation is based on contract, the logical relation between the cooperating individuals is symmetrical. They are all parties to interpersonal exchange contracts. John has the same relation to Tom as Tom has to John. Where and as far as cooperation is based on command and subordination, there is the man who commands and there are those who obey his orders. The logical relation between these two classes of men is asymmetrical. There is a director and there are people under his care. The director alone chooses and directs; the others – the wards – are mere pawns in his actions. [10,2]

In the frame of a contractual society the individual members exchange definite quantities of goods and services of a definite quality. In choosing subjection in a hegemonic body a man neither gives nor receives anything that is definite. He integrates himself into a system in which he has to render indefinite services and will receive what the director is willing to assign to him. He is at the mercy of the director. The director alone is free to choose. Whether the director is an individual or an organized group of individuals, a directorate, and whether the director is a selfish maniacal tyrant or a benevolent paternal despot is of no relevance for the structure of the whole system. [10,2]

The contractual order of society is an order of right and law. It is a government under the rule of law (Rechtsstaat) as differentiated from the welfare state (Wohlfahrtsstaat) or paternal state. Right or law is the complex of rules determining the orbit in which individuals are free to act. No such orbit is left to wards of a hegemonic society. In the hegemonic state there is neither right nor law; there are only directives and regulations which the director may change daily and apply with what discrimination he pleases and which the wards must obey. The wards have one freedom only: to obey without asking questions. [10,2]

The government

In order to establish and to preserve social cooperation and civilization, measures are needed to prevent asocial indi-

viduals from committing acts that are bound to undo all that
man has accomplished in his progress from the Neanderthal
level. In order to preserve the state of affairs in which there is
protection of the individual against the unlimited tyranny of
stronger and smarter fellows, an institution is needed that
curbs all antisocial elements. Peace – the absence of perpetual
fighting by everyone against everyone – can be attained only by
the establishment of a system in which the power to resort to
violent action is monopolized by a social apparatus of compulsion and coercion and the application of this power in any individual case is regulated by a set of rules – the man-made laws
as distinguished both from the laws of nature and those of
praxeology. The essential implement of a social system is the
operation of such an apparatus commonly called government.
[15,6]

State or government is the social apparatus of compulsion and coercion. It has the monopoly of violent action. No
individual is free to use violence or the threat of violence if the
government has not accorded this right to him. The state is essentially an institution for the preservation of peaceful interhuman relations. However, for the preservation of peace it must
be prepared to crush the onslaughts of peace-breakers. [8,2]

The concepts of freedom and bondage make sense only
when referring to the way in which government operates. It
would be highly inexpedient and misleading to say that a man
is not free because, if he wants to stay alive, his power to
choose between a drink of water and one of potassium cyanide
is restricted by nature. It would be no less inconvenient to call
a man unfree because the law imposes sanctions upon his desire to kill another man and because the police and the penal
courts enforce them. As far as the government – the social apparatus of compulsion and oppression – confines the exercise
of its violence and the threat of such violence to the suppression and prevention of antisocial action, there prevails what
reasonably and meaningfully can be called liberty. What is restrained is merely conduct that is bound to disintegrate social
cooperation and civilization, thus throwing all people back to
conditions that existed at the time homo sapiens emerged from
the purely animal existence of its nonhuman ancestors. Such

coercion does not substantially restrict man's power to choose. Even if there were no government enforcing man-made laws, the individual could not have both the advantages derived from the existence of social cooperation on the one hand, and, on the other, the pleasures of freely indulging in the rapacious animal instincts of aggression. [15,6]

In the market economy, the laissez-faire type of social organization, there is a sphere within which the individual is free to choose between various modes of acting without being restrained by the threat of being punished. If, however, the government does more than protect people against violent or fraudulent aggression on the part of antisocial individuals, it reduces the sphere of the individual's freedom to act beyond the degree to which it is restricted by praxeological law. Thus we may define freedom as that state of affairs in which the individual's discretion to choose is not constrained by governmental violence beyond the margin within which the praxeological law restricts it anyway. [15,6]

Liberty and freedom are the conditions of man within a contractual society. Social cooperation under a system of private ownership of the factors of production means that within the range of the market the individual is not bound to obey and to serve an overlord. As far as he gives and serves other people, he does so of his own accord in order to be rewarded and served by the receivers. He exchanges goods and services, he does not do compulsory labor and does not pay tribute. He is certainly not independent. He depends on the other members of society. But this dependence is mutual. The buyer depends on the seller and the seller on the buyer. [15,6]

Every step a government takes beyond the fulfillment of its essential functions of protecting the smooth operation of the market economy against aggression, whether on the part of domestic or foreign disturbers, is a step forward on a road that directly leads into the totalitarian system where there is no freedom at all. [15,6]

No government and no civil law can guarantee and bring about freedom otherwise than by supporting and defending the fundamental institutions of the market economy. Government means always coercion and compulsion and is by necessity the opposite of liberty. Government is a guarantor of liberty and is compatible with liberty only if its range is adequately restricted to the preservation of what is called economic freedom. Where there is no market economy, the best-intentioned provisions of constitutions and laws remain a dead letter. [15,6]

The nature of government intervention

The intervention is a decree issued directly or indirectly, by the authority in charge of society's administrative apparatus of coercion and compulsion which forces the entrepreneurs and capitalists to employ some of the factors of production in a way different from what they would have resorted to if they were only obeying the dictates of the market. Such a decree can be either an order to do something or an order not to do something. It is not required that the decree be issued directly by the established and generally recognized authority itself. It may happen that some other agencies arrogate to themselves the power to issue such orders or prohibitions and to enforce them by an apparatus of violent coercion and oppression of their own. If the recognized government tolerates such procedures or even supports them by the employment of its governmental police apparatus, matters stand as if the government itself had acted. If the government is opposed to other agencies' violent action, but does not succeed in suppressing it by means of its own armed forces, although it would like to suppress it, anarchy results. [27,2]

It is important to remember that government interference always means either violent action or the threat of such action. The funds that a government spends for whatever purposes are levied by taxation. And taxes are paid because the taxpayers are afraid of offering resistance to the tax gatherers. They know that any disobedience or resistance is hopeless. As long as this is the state of affairs, the government is able to collect the money that it wants to spend. Government is in the last resort the employment of armed men, of policemen, gendarmes, soldiers, prison guards, and hangmen. The essential feature of government is the enforcement of its decrees by beating, killing, and imprisoning. Those who are asking for more government interference are asking ultimately for more compulsion and less freedom. [27,2]

To draw attention to this fact does not imply any reflection upon government activities. In stark reality, peaceful social cooperation is impossible if no provision is made for violent prevention and suppression of antisocial action on the part of refractory individuals and groups of individuals. One must take exception to the often-repeated phrase that government is an evil, although a necessary and indispensable evil. What is required for the attainment of an end is a means, the cost to be expended for its successful realization. It is an arbitrary value judgment to describe it as an evil in the moral connotation of the term. However, in face of the modern tendencies toward a deification of government and state, it is good to remind ourselves that the old Romans were more realistic in symbolizing the state by a bundle of rods with an ax in the middle than are our contemporaries in ascribing to the state all the attributes of God. [27,2]

State and government are not ends, but means. Inflicting evil upon other people is a source of direct pleasure only to sadists. Established authorities resort to coercion and compulsion in order to safeguard the smooth operation of a definite system of social organization. The sphere in which coercion and compulsion is applied and the content of the laws which are to be enforced by the police apparatus are conditioned by the social order adopted. As state and government are designed to make this social system operate safely, the delimitation of governmental functions must be adjusted to its requirements. The only standard for the appreciation of the laws and the methods for their enforcement is whether or not they are efficient in safeguarding the social order which it is desired to preserve. [27,3]

The problem of interventionism is not a problem of the correct delimitation of the "natural," "just," and "proper" tasks of state and government. The issue is: How does a system of interventionism work? Can it realize those ends which people, in resorting to it, want to attain? [27,3]

If it is in the jurisdiction of the government to decide whether or not definite conditions of the economy justify its intervention, no sphere of operation is left to the market. Then it is no longer the consumers who ultimately determine what should be produced, in what quantity, of what quality, by whom, where, and how – but it is the government. For as soon as the outcome brought about by the operation of the unhampered market differs from what the authorities consider "socially" desirable, the government interferes. That means the market is free as long as it does precisely what the government wants it to do. It is "free" to do what the authorities consider to be the "right" things, but not to do what they consider the "wrong" things; the decision concerning what is right and what is wrong rests with the government. Thus the doctrine and the practice of interventionism ultimately tend to abandon what originally distinguished them from outright socialism and to adopt entirely the principles of totalitarian all-round planning. [27,3]

Taxation

To keep the social apparatus of coercion and compulsion running requires expenditure of labor and commodities. Under a liberal system of government these expenditures are small compared with the sum of the individuals' incomes. The more the government expands the sphere of its activities, the more its budget increases. [28,1]

The neutral tax would affect the conditions of the citizens only to the extent required by the fact that a part of the labor and material goods available is absorbed by the government apparatus. In the imaginary construction of the evenly rotating economy the treasury continually levies taxes and spends the whole amount raised, neither more nor less, for defraying the costs incurred by the activities of the government's officers. A part of each citizen's income is spent for public expenditure. If we assume that in such an evenly rotating economy there prevails perfect income equality in such a way that every household's income is proportional to the number of its members, both a head tax and a proportional income tax would be neutral taxes. Under these assumptions there would be no difference between them. A part of each citizen's income would be absorbed by public expenditure, and no secondary effects of taxation would emerge. [28,1]

The changing economy is entirely different from this imaginary construction of an evenly rotating economy with income equality. Continuous change and the inequality of wealth and income are essential and necessary features of the changing market economy, the only real and working system of the market economy. In the frame of such a system no tax can be neutral. The very idea of a neutral tax is as unrealizable as that of neutral money. But, of course, the reasons for this inescapable non-neutrality are different in the case of taxes from what they are in the case of money. [28,1]

Taxation is a matter of the market economy. It is one of the characteristic features of the market economy that the government does not interfere with the market phenomena and that its technical apparatus is so small that its maintenance absorbs only a modest fraction of the total sum of the individual citizens' incomes. Then taxes are an appropriate vehicle for providing the funds needed by the government. They are appropriate because they are low and do not perceptibly disarrange production and consumption. If taxes grow beyond a moderate limit, they cease to be taxes and turn into devices for the destruction of the market economy. [28,3]

Restriction of production

Restriction of production means that the government either forbids or makes more difficult or more expensive the production, transportation, or distribution of definite articles, or the application of definite modes of production, transportation, or distribution. The authority thus eliminates some of the means available for the satisfaction of human wants. The effect of its interference is that people are prevented from using their knowledge and abilities, their labor and their material means of production in the way in which they would earn the highest returns and satisfy their needs as much as possible. Such interference makes people poorer and less satisfied. [29,1]

In enacting restrictive measures governments and parliaments have hardly ever been aware of the consequences of their meddling with business. Thus, they have blithely assumed that protective tariffs are capable of raising the nation's standard of living, and they have stubbornly refused to admit the correctness of the economic teachings concerning the effects of protectionism. The economists' condemnation of protectionism is irrefutable and free of any party bias. For the economists do not say that protection is bad from any preconceived point of view. They show that protection cannot attain those ends which the governments as a rule want to attain by resorting to it. They do not question the ultimate end of the government's action; they merely reject the means chosen as inappropriate to realize the ends aimed at. [29,2]

Every disarrangement of the market data affects various individuals and groups of individuals in a different way. For some people it is a boon, for others a blow. Only after a while, when production is adjusted to the emergence of the new datum, are these effects exhausted. Thus a restrictive measure, while placing the immense majority at a disadvantage, may temporarily improve some people's position. For those favored the measure is tantamount to the acquisition of a privilege. They are asking for such measures because they want to be privileged. [29,3]

Here again the most striking example is provided by protectionism. The imposition of a duty on the importation of a commodity burdens the consumers. But to the domestic producers it is a boon. From their point of view decreeing new tariffs and raising already existing tariffs is an excellent thing. [29,3]

There are, as has been shown, cases in which a restrictive measure can attain the end sought by its application. If those resorting to such a measure think that the attainment of this goal is more important than the disadvantages brought about by the restriction – i.e., the curtailment in the quantity of material goods available for consumption – the recourse to restriction is justified from the point of view of their value judgments. They incur costs and pay a price in order to get something that they value more than what they had to expend or to forego. Nobody, and certainly not the theorist, is in a position to argue with them about the propriety of their value judgments. [29,4]

The only adequate mode of dealing with measures restricting production is to look at them as sacrifices made for the attainment of a definite end. They are quasi-expenditures and quasi-consumption. They are an employment of things that could be produced and consumed in one way for the realization of certain other ends. These things are prevented from coming into existence, but this quasi-consumption is precisely what satisfies the authors of these measures better than the increase in goods available which the omission of the restriction would have produced. [29,4]

Economics does not contend that restriction is a bad system of production. It asserts that it is not at all a system of production but rather a system of quasi-consumption. Most of the ends the interventionists want to attain by restriction cannot be attained this way. But even where restrictive measures are fit to attain the ends sought, they are only restrictive. [29,4]

The enormous popularity which restriction enjoys in our day is due to the fact that people do not recognize its consequences. In dealing with the problem of shortening the hours of work by government decree, the public is not aware of the fact that total output must drop and that it is very probable that the wage earners' standard of living will be potentially lowered too. It is a dogma of present-day "unorthodoxy" that such a "prolabor" measure is a "social gain" for the workers and that the costs of these gains fall entirely upon the employers. Whoever questions this dogma is branded as a "sycophantic" apologist of the unfair pretensions of rugged exploiters, and pitilessly persecuted. It is insinuated that he wants to reduce the wage earners to the poverty and the long working hours of the early stages of modern industrialism. [29,4]

Government interference in prices

Interference with the structure of the market means that the authority aims at fixing prices for commodities and services and interest rates at a height different from what the unhampered market would have determined. It decrees, or empowers – either tacitly or expressly – definite groups of people to decree, prices and rates which are to be considered either as maxima or as minima, and it provides for the enforcement of such decrees by coercion and compulsion. [30,1]

In resorting to such measures the government wants to favor either the buyer – as in the case of maximum prices – or the seller – as in the case of minimum prices. The maximum price is designed to make it possible for the buyer to procure what he wants at a price lower than that of the unhampered market. The minimum price is designed to make it possible for the seller to dispose of his merchandise or his services at a price higher than that of the unhampered market. It depends on the political balance of forces which groups the authority wants to favor. At times governments have resorted to maximum prices, at other times to minimum prices for various commodities. At times they have decreed maximum wage rates, at other times minimum wage rates. It is only with regard to interest that they have never had recourse to minimum rates; when they have interfered, they have always decreed maximum interest rates. They have always looked askance upon saving, investing, and moneylending. [30,1]

The characteristic feature of the market price is that it tends to equalize supply and demand. The size of the demand coincides with the size of supply not only in the imaginary construction of the evenly rotating economy. The notion of the plain state of rest as developed by the elementary theory of prices is a faithful description of what come to pass in the market at every instant. Any deviation of a market price from the height at which supply and demand are equal is – in the unhampered market – self-liquidating. [30,2]

But if the government fixes prices at a height different from what the market would have fixed if left alone, this equilibrium of demand and supply is disturbed. Then there are – with maximum prices – potential buyers who cannot buy although they are ready to pay the price fixed by the authority, or even a higher price. Then there are – with minimum prices – potential sellers who cannot sell although they are ready to sell at the price fixed by the authority, or even at a lower price. The price can no longer segregate those potential buyers and sellers who can buy or sell from those who cannot. A different principle for the allocation of the goods and services concerned and for the selection of those who are to receive portions of the supply available necessarily comes into operation. It may be that only those are in a position to buy who come first, or only those to whom particular circumstances (such as personal connections) assign a privileged position, or only those ruthless fellows who chase away their rivals by resorting to intimidation or violence. If the authority does not want chance or violence to determine the allocation of the supply available and conditions to become chaotic, it must itself regulate the amount which each individual is permitted to buy. It must resort to rationing. [30,2]

But rationing does not affect the core of the issue. The allocation of portions of the supply already produced and available to the various individuals eager to obtain a quantity of the goods concerned is only a secondary function of the market. Its primary function is the direction of production. It directs the employment of the factors of production into those channels in which they satisfy the most urgent needs of the consumers. If the government's price ceiling refers only to one consumers' good or to a limited amount of consumers' goods while the prices of the complementary factors of production are left free, production of the consumers' goods concerned will drop. The marginal producers will discontinue producing them lest they suffer losses. The not absolutely specific factors of production will be employed to a greater extent for the production of other goods not subject to price ceilings. A greater part of the absolutely specific factors of production will remain unused than would have remained in the absence of price ceilings. There emerges a tendency to shift production activities from the production of the goods affected by the maximum prices into the production of other goods. This outcome is, however, manifestly contrary to the intentions of the government. In resorting to price ceilings the authority wanted to make the commodities concerned more easily accessible to the consumers. It considered precisely those commodities so vital that it singled them out for a special measure in order to make it possible even for poor people to be amply supplied with them. But the result of the government's interference is that production of these commodities drops or stops altogether. It is a complete failure. [30,2]

It would be vain for the government to try to remove these undesired consequences by decreeing maximum prices likewise for the factors of production needed for the production of the consumers' goods the prices of which it has fixed. Such a measure would be successful only if all factors of production required were absolutely specific. As this can never be the case, the government must add to its first measure, fixing the price of only one consumers' good below the potential market price, more and more price ceilings, not only for all other consumers' goods and for all material factors of production, but no less for labor. It must compel every entrepreneur, capitalist, and employee to continue producing at the prices, wage rates, and interest rates which the government has fixed, to produce those quantities which the government orders them to produce, and to sell the products to those people – producers or consumers – whom the government determines. If one branch of production were to be exempt from this regimentation, capital and labor would flow into it; production would be restricted precisely in those other – regimented – branches which the government considered so important that it interfered with the conduct of their affairs. [30,2]

Economics does not say that isolated government interference with the prices of only one commodity or a few commodities is unfair, bad, or unfeasible. It says that such interference produces results contrary to its purpose, that it makes conditions worse, not better, from the point of view of the government and those backing its interference. Before the government interfered, the goods concerned were, in the eyes of the government, too dear. As a result of the maximum price their supply dwindles or disappears altogether. The government interfered because it considered these commodities especially vital, necessary, indispensable. But its action curtailed the supply available. It is therefore, from the point of view of the government, absurd and nonsensical. [30,2]

Freedom and laissez-faire

The freedom of man under capitalism is an effect of competition. The worker does not depend on the good graces of an employer. If his employer discharges him, he finds another employer. The consumer is not at the mercy of the shopkeeper. He is free to patronize another shop if he likes. Nobody must kiss other people's hands or fear their disfavor. Interpersonal relations are businesslike. the exchange of goods and services is mutual; it is not a favor to sell or to buy, it is a transaction dictated by selfishness on either side. [15,6]

It is true that in his capacity as a producer every man depends either directly − e.g., the entrepreneur − or indirectly − e.g., the hired worker − on the demands of the consumers. However, this dependence upon the supremacy of the consumers is not unlimited. If a man has a weighty reason for defying the sovereignty of the consumers, he can try it. There is in the range of the market a very substantial and effective right to resist oppression. Nobody is forced to go into the liquor industry or into a gun factory if his conscience objects. He may have to pay a price for his conviction; there are in this world no ends the attainment of which is gratuitous. But it is left to a man's own decision to choose between a material advantage and the call of what he believes to be his duty. In the market economy the individual alone is the supreme arbiter in matters of his satisfaction. [15,6]

Capitalist society has no means of compelling a man to change his occupation or his place of work other than to reward those complying with the wants of the consumers by higher pay. It is precisely this kind of pressure which many people consider as unbearable and hope to see abolished under socialism. They are too dull to realize that the only alternative is to convey to the authorities full power to determine in what branch and at what place a man should work. [15,6]

In his capacity as consumer man is no less free. He alone decides what is more and what is less important for him. He chooses how to spend his money according to his own will. [15,6]

The substitution of economic planning for the market economy removes all freedom and leaves to the individual merely the right to obey. The authority directing all economic matters controls all aspects of a man's life and activities. It is the only employer. All labor becomes compulsory labor because the employee must accept what the chief deigns to offer him. The economic tsar determines what and how much of each the consumer may consume. There is no sector of human life in which a decision is left to the individual's value judgments. The authority assigns a definite task to him, trains him for his job, and employs him at the place and in the manner it deems expedient. [15,6]

As the interventionist sees things, the alternative is "automatic forces" or "conscious planning." It is obvious, he implies, that to rely upon automatic processes is sheer stupidity. No reasonable man can seriously recommend doing nothing and letting things go as they do without interference on the part of purposive action. A plan, by the very fact that it is a display of conscious action, is incomparably superior to the absence of any planning. Laissez faire is said to mean: Let the evils last, do not try to improve the lot of mankind by reasonable action. [27,5]

The truth is that the alternative is not between a dead mechanism or a rigid automatism on one hand and conscious planning on the other hand. The alternative is not plan or no plan. The question is whose planning? Should each member of society plan for himself, or should a benevolent government alone plan for them all? The issue is not automatism versus conscious action; it is autonomous action of each individual versus the exclusive action of the government. It is freedom versus government omnipotence. [27,5]

Laissez faire does not mean: Let soulless mechanical forces operate. It means: Let each individual choose how he wants to cooperate in the social division of labor; let the consumers determine what the entrepreneurs should produce. Planning means: Let the government alone choose and enforce its rulings by the apparatus of coercion and compulsion. [27,5]

Laissez faire means: Let the common man choose and act; do not force him to yield to a dictator. [27,5]

As soon as the economic freedom which the market economy grants to its members is removed, all political liberties and bills of rights become humbug. Habeas corpus and trial by jury are a sham if, under the pretext of economic expediency, the authority has full power to relegate every citizen it dislikes to the arctic or to a desert and to assign him "hard labor" for life. Freedom of the press is a mere blind if the authority controls all printing offices and paper plants. And so are all the other rights of men. [15,6]

Praxeology and liberalism[11]

As a political doctrine liberalism is not neutral with regard to values and the ultimate ends sought by action. It assumes that all men or at least the majority of people are intent upon attaining certain goals. It gives them information about the means suitable to the realization of their plans. The champions of liberal doctrines are fully aware of the fact that their teachings are valid only for people who are committed to these valuational principles. [8,2]

While praxeology, and therefore economics too, uses the terms happiness and removal of uneasiness in a purely formal sense, liberalism attaches to them a concrete meaning. It presupposes that people prefer life to death, health to sickness, nourishment to starvation, abundance to poverty. It teaches man how to act in accordance with these valuations. [8,2]

It is customary to call these concerns materialistic and to charge liberalism with an alleged crude materialism and a neglect of the "higher" and "nobler" pursuits of mankind. Man does not live by bread alone, say the critics, and they disparage

11 "liberalism" is used in its original; meaning: a doctrine of maximum individual freedom and minimal government intervention. Usage of the word "liberalism" in English-speaking countries has been perverted, and the doctrine of individual freedom is now called "classical liberalism" or, in its extreme form, "libertarianism".

the meanness and despicable baseness of the utilitarian philosophy. However, these passionate diatribes are wrong because they badly distort the teachings of liberalism. [8,2]

First: The liberals do not assert that men ought to strive after the goals mentioned above. What they maintain is that the immense majority prefer a life of health and abundance to misery, starvation, and death. The correctness of this statement cannot be challenged. It is proved by the fact that all antiliberal doctrines – the theocratic tenets of the various religious, statist, nationalist, and socialist parties – adopt the same attitude with regard to these issues. They all promise their followers a life of plenty. They have never ventured to tell people that the realization of their program will impair their material well-being. They insist – on the contrary – that while the realization of the plans of their rival parties will result in indigence for the majority, they themselves want to provide their supporters with abundance. The Christian parties are no less eager in promising the masses a higher standard of living than the nationalists and the socialists. Present-day churches often speak more about raising wage rates and farm incomes than about the dogmas of the Christian doctrine. [8,2]

Secondly: The liberals do not disdain the intellectual and spiritual aspirations of man. On the contrary. They are prompted by a passionate ardor for intellectual and moral perfection, for wisdom and for aesthetic excellence. But their view of these high and noble things is far from the crude representations of their adversaries. They do not share the naive opinion that any system of social organization can directly succeed in encouraging philosophical or scientific thinking, in producing masterpieces of art and literature and in rendering the masses more enlightened. They realize that all that society can achieve in these fields is to provide an environment which does not put insurmountable obstacles in the way of the genius and makes the common man free enough from material concerns to become interested in things other than mere breadwinning. In their opinion the foremost social means of making man more human is to fight poverty. Wisdom and science and the arts thrive better in a world of affluence than among needy peoples. [8,2]

The quasi-theological character of all collectivist doctrines becomes manifest in their mutual conflicts. A collectivist doctrine does not assert the superiority of a collective whole in abstracto; it always proclaims the eminence of a definite collectivist idol, and either flatly denies the existence of other such idols or relegates them to a subordinate and ancillary position with regard to its own idol. The worshipers of the state proclaim the excellence of a definite state, i.e., their own; the nationalists, the excellence of their own nation. If dissenters challenge their particular program by heralding the superiority of another collectivist idol, they resort to no objection other than to declare again and again : We are right because an inner voice tells us that we are right and you are wrong. The conflicts of antagonistic collectivist creeds and sects cannot be decided by ratiocination; they must be decided by arms. The alternatives to the liberal and democratic principle of majority rule are the militarist principles of armed conflict and dictatorial oppression. [8,2]

The customary terminology misrepresents these things entirely. The philosophy commonly called individualism is a philosophy of social cooperation and the progressive intensification of the social nexus. On the other hand the application of the basic ideas of collectivism cannot result in anything but social disintegration and the perpetuation of armed conflict. It is true that every variety of collectivism promises eternal peace starting with the day of its own decisive victory and the final overthrow and extermination of all other ideologies and their supporters. However, the realization of these plans is conditioned upon a radical transformation in mankind. Men must be divided into two classes: the omnipotent godlike dictator on the one hand and the masses which must surrender volition and reasoning in order to become mere chessmen in the plans of the dictator. The masses must be dehumanized in order to make one man their godlike master. Thinking and acting, the foremost characteristics of man as man, would become the privilege of one man only. [8,2]

The liberals do not maintain that majorities are godlike and infallible; they do not contend that the mere fact that a policy is advocated by the many is a proof of its merits for the common weal. They do not recommend the dictatorship of the majority and the violent oppression of dissenting minorities. Liberalism aims at a political constitution which safeguards the smooth working of social cooperation and the progressive intensification of mutual social relations. Its main objective is the avoidance of violent conflicts, of wars and revolutions that must disintegrate the social collaboration of men and throw people back into the primitive conditions of barbarism where all tribes and political bodies endlessly fought one another. Because the division of labor requires undisturbed peace, liberalism aims at the establishment of a system of government that is likely to preserve peace, viz., democracy. [8,2]

Liberalism and religion

Liberalism is based upon a purely rational and scientific theory of social cooperation. The policies it recommends are the application of a system of knowledge which does not refer in any way to sentiments, intuitive creeds for which no logically sufficient proof can be provided, mystical experiences, and the personal awareness of superhuman phenomena. In this sense the often misunderstood and erroneously interpreted epithets atheistic and agnostic can be attributed to it. It would, however, be a serious mistake to conclude that the sciences of human action and the policy derived from their teachings, liberalism, are antitheistic and hostile to religion. They are radically opposed to all systems of theocracy. But they are entirely neutral with regard to religious beliefs which do not pretend to interfere with the conduct of social, political, and economic affairs. [8,2]

Theocracy is a social system which lays claim to a superhuman title for its legitimation. The fundamental law of a theocratic regime is an insight not open to examination by reason and to demonstration by logical methods. Its ultimate standard is intuition providing the mind with subjective certainty about things which cannot be conceived by reason and ratiocination. If this intuition refers to one of the traditional systems of teaching concerning the existence of a Divine Creator and Ruler of the universe, we call it a religious belief. If it refers to another system we call it a metaphysical belief. Thus a system of theocratic government need not be founded on one of the great historical religions of the world. It may be the outcome of metaphysical tenets which reject all traditional churches and denominations and take pride in emphasizing their antitheistic and antimetaphysical character. [8,2]

Liberalism puts no obstacles in the way of a man eager to adjust his personal conduct and his private affairs according to the mode in which he individually or his church or denomination interprets the teachings of the Gospels. But it is radically opposed to all endeavors to silence the rational discussion of problems of social welfare by an appeal to religious intuition and revelation. It does not enjoin divorce or the practice of birth control upon anybody. But it fights those who want to prevent other people from freely discussing the pros and cons of these matters. [8,2]

In the liberal opinion the aim of the moral law is to impel individuals to adjust their conduct to the requirements of life in society, to abstain from all acts detrimental to the preservation of peaceful social cooperation and to the improvement of interhuman relations. Liberals welcome the support which religious teachings may give to those moral precepts of which they themselves approve, but they are opposed to all those norms which are bound to bring about social disintegration from whatever source they may stem. [8,2]

It is a distortion of fact to say, as many champions of religious theocracy do, that liberalism fights religion. Where the principle of church interference with secular issues is in force, the various churches, denominations and sects are fighting one another. By separating church and state, liberalism establishes peace between the various religious factions and gives to each of them the opportunity to preach its gospel unmolested. [8,2]

Liberalism is rationalistic. It maintains that it is possible to convince the immense majority that peaceful cooperation within the framework of society better serves their rightly understood interests than mutual battling and social disintegration. It has full confidence in man's reason. It may be that this optimism is unfounded and that the liberals have erred. But then there is no hope left for mankind's future. [8,2]

IF YOU LIKED THIS BOOK

please recommend it to your friends
and associates

and leave a comment on the Amazon site

author contact :
gdrean@sfr.fr

Printed by CreateSpace
An Amazon.com Company

Available from Amazon.com
and other retail outlets